Writing for Young People

HAZEL EDWARDS

Writing for Young People

Second Edition

Acknowledgement

Goldie Alexander contributed to the first edition. She wrote historical fiction such as *My Australian Story: Surviving Sydney Cove* and her *Mentoring Your Memoir* was used by many family historians as a 'how-to write' text.

Published in 2023 by Amba Press, Melbourne, Australia.
www.ambapress.com.au

© Hazel Edwards 2023

All rights reserved. No part of this book may be reproduced or transmitted in any form or by any means, electronic or mechanical, including photocopying, recording or by any information storage and retrieval system, without prior permission in writing from the publisher.

This book was first published in 1998 by Hale & Iremonger Pty Ltd.

Cover design: Tess McCabe
Proofreader: Jason Chandra

ISBN: 9781922607867 (pbk)
ISBN: 9781922607874 (ebk)

A catalogue record for this book is available from the National Library of Australia.

Contents

Introduction	1
Chapter 1: Preparing to be a writer	3
Writing for the children's book market	3
Keep contact with potential reader's interests	4
Monitor literary trends	5
Research the market	5
Set up a home office and time to write	6
Take ideas from different mediums	6
Sequence of writing a book	6
Value of children's bookshops	7
Exercises	8
Checklist	8
Chapter 2: Starting up a business	11
Establishing your audience	11
Stay informed with relevant topics	12
Use existing areas of expertise	12
Creating stories from real life experiences	12
Keep a writer's notebook	13
Clip files and research	14
Networking for writers	14
Helpful hints	14
Exercises	16
Checklist	17

Chapter 3: Selling a manuscript — 19

    Research the market — 19
    Writing book proposals — 19
    Writing synopses — 20
    Organising a series — 23
    Exercises — 27
    Checklist — 27

Chapter 4: Genres — 29

    Definitions — 29
    Differing kinds of genres — 30
    Writing romance — 31
    Exercise — 34
    Checklist — 34

Chapter 5: Business plans — 37

    Attitude: Amateur or professional — 37
    Establish a timetable — 37
    Projected income — 37
    General stages of writing as a career — 38
    Handling different projects — 39
    Keep an open mind — 39
    Observe the opposition — 39
    Use the Internet — 39
    Handling stress — 40
    Relevant business services — 40
    Business basics — 41
    Networking — 41
    Hints — 41
    Exercises — 42
    Checklist — 42

Chapter 6: Overcoming procrastination — 45

    Don't start at chapter 1 — 45
    Commit to a deadline — 45
    Switch between projects — 45

Keeping relaxed	46
Writer-in-residency	46
Exercises	48
Checklist	48

Chapter 7: Working with multimedia   49

Definitions	49
Practitioners' responses	51
Developing children's games	51
Working in animation	52
Creating an author website	53
Edutainment	53
Children's TV	54
Adaptation proposals: Picture book to stage production	54
How not to write for the latest medium	56
Exercises	58
Checklist	59

Chapter 8: Commercial scripting   61

Fostering interactivity with commercial scripting	61
TV scripting	62
FAQs of TV scripting	63
Other digital formats	64
Scripting for film	64
Scripting for puppet plays	65
Miming	65
Unusual scripting	66

Chapter 9: Educational scripting   67

Classroom scripts	67
Theatre in education	67
Scripting for audiobooks	68
Performance lyrics, rap and poetry	68
Shopping centres and street theatre	68
Hints for scripting plays	69
Scripting for documentaries	70
Novelisations	71

Fostering literacy with scripts — 71
Exercise — 72
Checklist — 73

Chapter 10: Crafting a story — 75

Crafting an intriguing plot — 75
Structure — 76
Creating your story's characters — 76
Creating a good opening — 77
Voice and viewpoint — 79
Language — 80
Dialogue — 80
Settings — 80
Outlining chapters — 81
Creating enticing endings — 81
Word limit — 82
Exercises — 83
Checklist — 83

Chapter 11: Non-fiction — 87

Why write and cater to the non-fiction market? — 87
Examples of non-fiction writing — 88
Arranging a table of content — 89
Examples of creating a table of contents — 90
Exercises — 92
Checklist — 92

Chapter 12: A good title sells — 95

Features of a good title — 95
Exercises — 97
Checklist — 97

Chapter 13: Reworking and writing drafts — 99

Clearing mental space — 99
Redrafting — 99
Helpful hints — 100

Exercises	101
Checklist	101

Chapter 14: Marketing — 103

Market research	103
Two types of marketing	103
Professional competence	103
Maintaining good practices	104
Marketing strategies	105
Creating a corporate image	106
Manuscript (MS) presentation	107
Exercises	109
Checklist	109

Chapter 15: Coping with rejection — 111

Receiving rejection from publishers	111
Strategies for coping	111
Self-publishing	112
Join a writing group	113
Ethical dilemmas	114
Exercises	116
Checklist	116

Chapter 16: Collaborating and ghosting — 119

Creating a successful collaboration	119
Aspects of unsuccessful collaborations	120
Collaborating online	121
Pointers for productive partnerships	121
Ghost writers	122
Exercise	123
Checklist	123

Chapter 17: Reviews, critics and the media — 125

Dealing with reviews, listings and critics	125
Blurbs	126
Learning to become media worthy	127

Websites and social media	127
Fan letters	128
Writer-on-location	130
Exercises	131
Checklist	131

Chapter 18: Agents and international sales — 133

Literary agents	133
International sales	135
Translations and foreign rights	136
Works which travel well	137
Merchandising	138
Electronic rights and IP	138
Professional help	138
Exercises	139
Checklist	139

Glossary: The A to Z of writing for young people — 141

Appendix — 143

Tips for school students writing their own books	143
A historical gift: Writing for children in your extended family	144

About the author — 147

Introduction

Authors need a good story to share, but also be aware of the changing media world in which their readers live. That's why educators who are working daily with youth of the age for which they want to write, are already researching. They know their potential readership. The challenge is to write well, in new formats, including visuals, with appropriate humour and NOT be earnestly boring.

Recently, formats have changed SO fast that even the words multimedia and multicultural have been superseded. AI has caused major disruption within the industry. Sensitivity readers are now required to make books more accessible. Cultural appropriation issues continue to occur.

Children's books emphasise writing in a businesslike but creatively satisfying way for adolescent audiences as well as your target community. Project planning, time and energy management, and markets are all covered in this book.

Many adult creators are seeking literary self-employment so proposals, examples, strategies and checklists, are provided. But the writing techniques are also relevant to share with child writers and illustrators too.

This book features:

- Relevant exercises
- Checklists at the end of each chapter
- Activities and lessons to be used by groups or individuals working in isolation
- Relevant materials that are used within tertiary writing courses.

"Creativity is the fun of putting together unexpected ideas"
– Hazel Edwards

CHAPTER 1

Preparing to be a writer

Writing for the children's book market

Writing for children is a technical challenge. Although the story should look easy to read, it has likely undergone countless revisions and drafts. Deceptive simplicity is the norm.

Being a children's author is more difficult than writing for adults. A child's response is immediate and honest. If the story is boring or fails to capture the child's imagination, the prospective listener or reader will yawn and tune out.

Competition is keen. Book authors vie with TV, computer games, digital entertainment and smart devices. Of course, the alternative option is to write for these mediums too. Being multi-skilled and adaptable is essential to thrive in the children's book business. Regardless of format, the ideas, visuals, and writing have to attract and retain the reader's interest.

Many teachers have transitioned to part-time or even full-time authors because of their familiarity with children's genuine interests.

So why do writers persist with their craft? Most writers write to be read, and they also write for themselves. Few writers earn a fortune, but the luxury of creativity can reap numerous rewards such as:

- Making imaginary worlds
- Presenting moral dilemmas

- Developing and emphasising characterisation
- Engaging the emotions
- Inventing exciting plots and settings.

Much is written about 'the book' becoming redundant. In the future, the story's means of presentation may alter – for example, digital readers in place of paper pages – but the content still needs to be created by authors and idea mongers, even in times of generative artificial intelligence (AI).

To help you focus on what sort of content works (and what doesn't) consider the following:.

- Do you have a favourite author? Think about any book you loved and read as a child. Why do you remember it?
- Was it because you could identify with the character's feelings?
- Did the story explore a situation with which you could empathise?
- Did it contain a heroic quest, standing up to bullies, talking to others, making friends?
- Did it help you cope in some other way? Were there times when you wanted to lose yourself in another world?
- Remember the reassurance felt from reading about others? The comfort of knowing you were not alone in an often-difficult world, knowing that you could gain vicarious experience from what you read, even if you didn't know what the word 'vicarious' meant then!
- Writing for children isn't a licence to preach, nor is it bibliotherapy. If you intend your story to carry a heavy moral message, this is propaganda, not children's literature.

Keep contact with potential reader's interests

Unless you are planning to write historical fiction set in the period when you grew up, with a character of your own gender, interests and hobby (which will save time and effort but for one story only), you will need to do some research.

Find out what children are currently interested in. Your own children might not be interested in the same typical things as other children. If you don't have any children, explore and do some investigation. Try to note down details about their lifestyles, hobbies, emotions, relationships, and dreams. All of these will be helpful in grasping a better understanding of your readers and what their needs are. Here are some tips to get you started:

- Talk and get to know children, e.g., your friends' children, not just your relatives.
- Listen very carefully to phrasing and content.
- Eavesdrop, but call it research.
- Read what contemporary writers are publishing.
- Find out what your target age group is reading and watching.
- Talk to your local librarian and bookseller.
- Watch children's TV programs.
- Research children's publishers through social media.
- Check which covers appeal to children.

Monitor literary trends

Real estate agents offer three pieces of advice: *Position. Position. Position.* For children's writers the advice is: *Read. Read. Read.* Good readers make better writers. By habitual osmosis you'll learn to incorporate style and technique.

Authors can also monitor literary trends among young people by staying engaged with popular social media platforms and actively participating in book communities. Paying attention to the themes, topics and writing styles that resonate with young readers allows authors to create relevant and compelling stories that connect with their target audience.

Research the market

Researching means not only gathering raw material for writing, it also means knowing what is being published and by whom. Don't confine your reading to the local scene. Think internationally. Writers need to know current trends, future possibilities and their own strengths.

Don't simply follow trends without careful consideration. For example, deciding to write horror because it's become a best-selling genre and trendy on BookTok is pointless if you dislike the genre.

Analyse and learn from changes occurring in books targeted at adults, because some of it will filter through to children's books. Embryonic stories can be shaped into more than one medium. Something successful in one medium may make it through to another, e.g., a picture book can be turned into a film and then adapted into a game or opera.

Set up a home office and time to write

Be serious about your intention to write. Too often potential authors are intimidated by lack of space or time. If you don't have your own study, *clear some space* in your bedroom, kitchen, laundry or garage. Invest in a laptop or iPad that lets you to work remotely from anywhere.

The matter of *time* is often harder to establish. People who have a compulsion to write will always find time, but those less obsessed may have to cut out other favoured activities. What about getting up an hour earlier? Using weekends? Writing while the family watches TV?

Take ideas from different mediums

Go through different mediums like newspapers, magazines, TV programs, online videos (i.e., YouTube, TikTok, Instagram) and films. You might consider writing for any of these mediums in the future. But if not, they can help you to understand and appreciate your audience's interests.

Consider browsing through educational websites for kids to get an insight as to what children are interested in. As media consumers, the youth draw and learn from other worldviews and languages. If you only want things to return to the way they were when you were a child, stick to writing historical fiction.

Sequence of writing a book

This is a simplified illustration of the process involved in writing a book:

- Brainstorming ideas
- Doing research
- Writing the first draft
- Making new drafts (i.e., 2–8 drafts, often more)
- Workshopping or trialling (feedback from peers)
- Rewriting drafts
- Final copy of draft (Digital and print copy)
- Publisher/editor's suggestions

- Rewriting and editing
- Illustrations including cover design
- Publication process
- Galleys to check
- Proofs to check
- Book launching (optional)
- Reviews
- Translation
- Other media e.g., TV, film, stage, comic graphic novel or audio-book.

Value of children's bookshops

Others go on pub crawls in their free time, but visiting specialty children's bookshops or going on library crawls will be of more immediate value in analysing market trends for a beginning writer. This can be either an in-person visit or through online browsing.

Dedicate spending a few hours in bookshops across several days or during the weekends. Generally, specialist bookshops tend to be run by enthusiasts. Take advantage of this and ask them any questions to help expand your knowledge.

Visit and write short notes (no more than two pages in total) on the special services or features offered at three specialist children's bookshops plus two other general bookshops of your choice. Consider:

- Availability of the most popular genres/titles/authors.
- How wide is their selection?
- Any noticeable trends? Titles? Covers? Display?
- How willing are they to follow up on elusive titles?
- Is the staff well informed on children's books?
- The length and tone of blurbs and author biographies – note your current favourites
- Is the physical setup appealing? Are there any small chairs or tables for young readers or is it adult-orientated?
- Apart from books, see if other materials are offered (e.g., audiobooks, apps, stickers, stamps or merchandising).
- Read book reviews online.
- Investigate toy lending libraries which also offer books to loan.
- Visit op shops to see which books have been discarded.

Exercises

1. Design an ideal situation for a writer in business.
2. Now modify this given the limitations of your personal lifestyle. Use the checklist below to help formulate your ideas.
3. Do a children's bookshop or library crawl, in person or online.

Checklist

1. Why are you writing books for children?

   _____
   _____
   _____

2. Where is your writing space set up?

   _____
   _____
   _____

3. What kind of digital device do you use/own?

   _____
   _____
   _____

4. List your planned writing times.

   _____
   _____
   _____

5. Have you arranged to contact children apart from your own? If yes, list down the time and dates.

    _____

    _____

    _____

    _____

6. Have you arranged any 'workshopping' sessions with your local school? If yes, list down the times and dates.

    _____

    _____

7. List all the contemporary children's books you have read this month.

Author	*Title*	*Publisher*	*Age Group*	*Genre*

8. Which library do you normally go to?

    _____

    _____

9. List any bookshops visited this month.

_____

_____

_____

10. List any children's TV program, theatre or film you have recently watched.

_____

_____

_____

11. Have you accessed any children's websites?

_____

_____

_____

12. Have you checked any streamed children's programs? E.g., Bluey.

_____

_____

_____

CHAPTER 2

Starting up a business

Establishing your audience

Who comes first? The audience or the writer? If you are contemplating selling your story, then the audience needs to come first. There are several factors you need to take into consideration to establish your audience, including:

- Story length
- Age group
- Vocabulary complexity
- Content
- Attention span
- Format presentation.

Will your idea use an established format or potentially a newer format? If you're unsure, look through existing formats and consider the differences and unique characteristics that might suit your idea:

- Fiction or non-fiction
- Poetry or performance pieces
- Song lyrics
- Plays, film, audio or interactive scripts
- Feature articles
- Photographs with captions
- Cartoons or animation.

A novel could be written in a 'novel' way, a way no one has attempted before. Some authors create a story then decide the target age group. Other writers prefer to be sparked by an idea or a theme. Then there are writers who choose a format, length, character and proceed from there.

Stay informed with relevant topics

Lots of kids are interested in sports, but authors tend to perpetuate the hobbies in which they're interested. So, there are a disproportionate number of child characters who love books and not many who like boxing, wrestling, soccer and bungee jumping.

Make an effort to research contemporary children's interests. Short of an idea? Take up windsurfing, dancing or skateboarding. No point in writing about what fascinated you as a child if it is now out of date. At least, not unless you make it into a mystery, ancient history or horror.

Research expenses, even for something as distinctive as hot air ballooning, are tax deductible for an author if the story earns income.

Use existing areas of expertise

Develop your skills at writing non-fiction. List six skills you already possess: e.g., dancing, jogging, organising parties, vegetarian shopping, cycling, horse-riding. Could you write about these without needing to do further research? Use familiar locations, think of a place you know that could make a dramatic setting. What previous occupations or lifestyles have you enjoyed? Could you give one of these to a character and make the details sound credible? How about using an embarrassing moment? Your *second* most embarrassing moment?

Creating stories from real life experiences

Some writers take freely from life. Others regard it as literary terrorism. Would you be insulted or complimented if someone recognised themselves in your character? How would you feel if a close friend 'fictionalised' a shared confidence or a traumatic event?

Writers inevitably must face this ethical dilemma. Taking real life experiences and using them to create stories warrants the dangers of a thinly disguised autobiography. 'Real life' is their research ground, however, a clever writer is able to meld various characteristics so that the result becomes fiction. A fictitious character is a composite which is more complex than any one person. A composite distils the essence of a character. Some of that essence may come from observation, eavesdropping or shared anecdotes from real life. But when this blends in the author's imagination, it emerges as a fresh character or situation.

The real danger in using real life situations, relatives and friends is that you might run out of material. And out of friends.

Keep a writer's notebook

Most writers keep a notebook where they jot down observations, thoughts and ideas. The less methodical have scattered pieces of paper, and the more tech-savvy use the latest audio device converting voice to text. Running a business means fast access to files, not wasting ideas and not spending hours searching for mislaid information. A good business is efficient.

In practical terms, what does this mean? Probably you will have to do everything yourself, so your system has to be simple. Have two or three (digital or other) folders labelled appropriately. Carry a notebook or a small recorder for ideas you think you will remember – and you forget. Keep an 'Ideas Folder' for screenshots or links. Keep business folders or email files for:

- Accounts, receipts, tax
- Researching publishers
- Recycling ideas
- Current books
- Fan mail
- PR and marketing materials.

Allocate an hour on late Friday afternoon, or some 'down' time, to handle accounts and the things you like least.

Remember, writing for children is similar to writing for any audience. You start with the same basic ingredients – *people, place, plot, problem, perspective* – just as you would in writing for adults, but the *presentation* will be different.

Clip files and research

Read newspapers for anecdotal ideas, often the 'odd spots' or the unusual paragraph can provide a setting or a twist to the end of a story. For example, a prediction about weather trends in the 22nd century can be used for fantasy, science fiction or mystery.

Screenshot or clip any headings and photos that provide inspiration. Date and annotate source, then retain them in a folder marked ideas. Use when necessary or desperate.

Networking for writers

It's essential to network with other writers and professionals in allied fields, such as photographers, illustrators, actors, storytellers, musicians or graphic designers. Often, they can offer you appropriate writing work to go with their ideas, or they may give a different slant to one of your ideas. One professional you should prioritise connecting with is with your local librarian. They will provide insider knowledge and can provide insightful feedback.

Utilise social networking sites. LinkedIn and Facebook are the most popular platform with a variety of groups you can join, but there are also a number of sites (e.g., Goodreads, The StoryGraph) that enable you to connect with other writers.

Connect with a specialist in every field, someone you can call quickly to check on facts or technical terms. Cultivating these connections will be mutually beneficial for you and your connections.

Utilise the Internet and find experts' sites exist where questions can be left.

Helpful hints

1. **Mentally choose a real person who fits your mythical audience.** Make sure that your piece is pitched to the person's age and interests, that the length, language level and design are relevant.
2. **Test your work and pitch it a bit lower.** Interest level and reading age may not be the same for some children. For example, 10-year-old Ben's reading skills are comparable to an 8-year-old. If the basketball

subject matter of your story interests him, and the words can be read by most 8-year-olds, he'll keep reading. But if the language level and sentence complexity is too challenging, he'll give up. Able readers cope with complex words if they're interested in the story.

3. **New readers need short sentences.** Find a child in the target age of your story. Invite that child to read a second copy aloud. Wherever they stumble, mark and edit your own copy. You'll soon find out if the subject and language interest them. Does your reader show curiosity in what happens next? Can they cope with any technical vocabulary? Are there too many characters who are not easily distinguished?

Exercises

1. Create 3 different short stories with the following prompt:

   Two children move to a new home. They are forced to combat a bully and make new friends.

   1st possible scenario:
   - The children are ants
   - The bully is a spider
   - The location is a child's bedroom.

   2nd possible scenario:
   - The children are both 12-year-olds
   - The bully is an Indice (indigenous to Mars, choose if they are an animal, vegetable or mineral)
   - The location is a Mars Hoverdrome.

   3rd possible scenario:
   - The boys are anthropomorphic red blood cells
   - The bully is a disease threat
   - The location is a living body.

2. Plot different stories using the following blurbs:

   BOY WONDER CRACKS BANK'S FILES

   Adam Ng, a 14-year-old secondary student, was apprehended by security on charges of hacking into bank files. When questioned, this young computer expert confessed that he did it for a dare. 'But it was dead easy,' young Adam Ng confessed. 'I found out a lot about the recruitment procedures for computer experts.' The bank refuses to comment but has offered Adam Ng some work experience.'

   TEENAGERS' NEW YEAR'S EVE BASH

   Two youths have been questioned by the police for brawling outside Galaxy Nightclub. The youths were accompanied by their girlfriends who claimed they were all 'best friends'.

   Magistrate Coralie Brown let them off with a severe warning about choosing friends more wisely.

Checklist

1. Who is your target audience?
   _____

2. What is the average age, interest and attention span?
   _____
   _____

3. In what ways are you creating stories that are too obviously from real life experiences?
   _____
   _____

4. In what ways are you keeping up to date with children's ideas and youthful interests?
   _____
   _____

5. Where in the story can you use your existing expertise?
   _____
   _____

6. Do you keep an ideas notebook or have created a clippings file?
   _____
   _____

7. With whom might you collaborate on a creative project?

_____

_____

8. How might you research your area of interest?

_____

_____

9. How well do you know your local library? Have you checked the junior reference section?

_____

_____

10. Have you experimented with a story in more than one format? If yes, what are your main takeaways and learning points?

_____

_____

_____

_____

CHAPTER 3

Selling a manuscript

Research the market

Before sending your book proposal to potential publishers, you need to familiarise yourself with the market that you're targeting. Conduct thorough research of the target market and follow standard practices:

- Browse new releases, reviews, bookshops and online sites for appropriate publishers.
- Get to know your local library and librarians.
- Attend authors' readings and launches.
- Observe international trends in the publishing industry.
- Join writers' organisations for the informal and formal marketing information.
- Keep an eye and ear on allied media.
- Consider unusual angles on current events for non-fiction article topics and book proposals.

Writing book proposals

A book proposal is one page which should include:

- Working title
- Potential audience
- Estimated completion date
- Synopsis
- Author biography

- Market profile
- Topicality
- Proposed length and deadline
- Sample chapter/s.

The aim is to convince the publisher that this book will be worth publishing. If this work is fiction indicate the central character, conflict, setting and genre. A non-fiction proposal should include a table of contents where chapter headings accurately indicate the contents.

A synopsis may also be used as part of a book proposal. This is a one-page outline of the novel. Sometimes a sample chapter will need to be included to indicate the writer's style.

A market profile can help you establish a list of similar books to your book idea. Distinguish the differences and similarities between competing books and yours. This provides the opportunity to show the potential publisher that your book is filling a gap in the market.

A book proposal is a time-management device for you and for the potential publisher. It forces you to assess a potential market and the opportunity. If a book takes up to a year in preparation, it is foolish to start without some realistic assessment.

Writing synopses

Usually no longer than one page, a synopsis gives the flavour of your book. It should be eloquently written, as the synopsis sells your book idea to the publisher. If the synopsis appeals, then the rest of the manuscript will be read. A synopsis entices and should seduce the publisher into wanting to know more.

Some authors write the synopsis first, and hope that it will entice a contract out of the publisher. Others write the synopsis after they finish the book. Either way, it must be written for an adult reader, and must be simple, clear and dramatic. Although a child will read the book, the language and sentence structure of the synopsis will always be read first by an adult.

Verb tenses

Some claim a synopsis should be written in the present tense because the manuscript continues to exist. Others claim it should be written in the past tense because it has been read. The major consideration is that the tense is consistent, so it is possible to write a synopsis in the present tense, even if the book is written in the past and vice versa.

Viewpoint

Generally, the third-person viewpoint is used because synopses are dispassionate and objective. In this way, it is possible to present more than one character and more than one perspective. Gushy strings of adjectives about 'this wonderful masterpiece' are best left to the blurb on the back cover and written 'in-house' by someone else.

Before or after?

Temperamentally, some authors enjoy the enforced discipline of structuring via the synopsis. Others dread being forced to outline a story which they know they will change in the writing. Some professionals willingly admit that when their publishers demand a synopsis in exchange for a contract, they write something that later bears little resemblance to the final book.

Elevator pitch

'Elevator pitch' is a slang term used to describe a brief speech that outlines an idea for a product, service, or project. Quicker than the time it takes to go up in an elevator to the next floor. Some publishers ask for a one sentence pitch. Practice writing an elevator pitch with your current manuscript.

Openings

Hook the publisher's readers by introducing the main character, establishing the setting and hinting at the conflict within the first couple of sentences.

Take a look into this example:

> *Astrid, the mind-reading chook, is a new-age, hard-boiled detective. Riding a Harley-Davidson with her mobile phone under one wing, she investigates her first case that involves finding the magician's lost sense of humour before his 3 p.m. shopping centre performance. Each time she has a good idea, she lays an egg.*

A writer will need to send a sample first chapter together with the synopsis, in order to gain a contract and an advance before going ahead with the project.

Sample synopsis for children's book

The following is a synopsis taken from the book *SkinZipped*:

> *Imagine being a see-through person.*
> *After too much sun, Edwina's skin peels off.*
> *Her skin has unzipped. But inside, she is the same.*
> *By mistake, her skin went in the wash.*
> *Unluckily, it shrank in the dryer.*
> *Friends can see her body working, inside.*
> *Especially when she eats beetroot or tomatoes.*
> *Doctors test Edwina.*
> *And filming the Giant Zips TV commercial is fun.*
> *Her fee goes to research.*
> *Inside, Edwina is just the same.*
> *In seven years, she'll have another skin.*
> *Meanwhile, she likes looking different.*

Sample blurb

The following is a blurb taken from the book *SkinZipped*:

> *How much does your skin matter?*
>
> *Edwina is a see-through 10-year-old. You can see her insides working.*
>
> *Too much sun means Edwina's skin came right off. Can she put it on again?*
>
> *What happens as she visits the medical and media worlds, with a see-through body and no skin colour?*
>
> *Is it a disability, diversity or fun?*

Skinzipped by Hazel Edwards was published digitally and is available from online bookstores like Amazon.

Sample synopsis for teens' literature

The following is a synopsis taken from the book *Misfit*:

> *What's an ordinary girl doing in a time-warped place where the boys wear black lids to keep their brains in?*
>
> *Crystal doesn't know how she's going to handle it, but it isn't the first time her parents have sent her to an unusual school. She's been to a Catholic School, Michael's Experimental, the ordinary Fernhill State, and to a hippie school. But in this school, all the kids are Jewish. She has to learn to decipher writing that looks like fly-dots and to find a way to speak to a whole new set of kids. Even Sharon, the bully.*
>
> *A story about cultural differences, kosher food, friendships, hockey, bullying and a miss who does fit, eventually.*
>
> *'Misfit' is set in Shalom, a fictional Australian Jewish school.*
>
> *When you look through a Crystal, you can see from different perspectives.*

Misfit by Hazel Edwards was published digitally and is available from online bookstores like Amazon.

Organising a series

Readers or publishers may 'read' a series differently. There is a difference between characters created for as *one-off* story which was so popular that sequels were requested, and one where a series was planned from the beginning. A story conceived for one medium such as a book, may be suited for screen, and this may be deliberately planned or just luck. Prequels and sequels may be requested.

Commercially, it makes sense to plan more than one title. The time and energy required to prepare a single book proposal for a publisher could be better spent on suggesting a series. When each new title is issued, this gives a boost to earlier ones, especially if there is a memorable overall title for the series. Merchandising of the character with soft toys, cards or games may also occur. But it can be frustrating if the publisher decides to stop after the first book. Often it is difficult to place concepts or books elsewhere. It is better to plan writing sequels after you receive confirmation via a contract.

Artistically, it is a challenge to create characters with sufficient depth or complexity to avoid readers becoming bored with the character. Being type-cast as the creator of a popular character or book series may limit the author's future opportunities to create new works.

A series editor or author may plan the treatment or synopses of the stories and provide the character outlines, but the individual stories may be written by different writers. Some series may be group-devised by several writers, especially in non-writing areas.

Mysteries or adventures are especially suited to series because the conflict is often external to the character, it is a problem of something lost or a mix-up that provides the story's drama. Mysteries tend to be plot-driven rather than character-driven and it's easier to place the stories in a variety of settings.

Initial scenarios need to be open-ended with credible reasons for the characters to move to a variety of locations, for events to occur and for new people to arrive.

Researching new backgrounds, processes or places provides a 'freshness' for the writer and reader.

Characters often take on lives of their own. Readers become very fond of the tiny details of their favourite characters' lives and so the creator must be careful not to forget minor details between stories e.g., the name Wilhemina was transposed to Henrietta as the goat's name in the Frequent Flyer Twins series. Luckily it was picked up during the trialling of the draft manuscript.

Characters must grow and yet remain recognisably the same. Often, they cannot have regular birthdays or they will become too 'old'. Authors must check on the period of their stories.

Easily recognisable cover design and titles are needed. Control over adaptation into other media and merchandising to retain the original concept may be necessary.

Technical challenges for authors

There are important aspects that authors need to keep in mind when creating a series:

- Do characters remain the same age?
- What timespan will be covered in the story?
- Keeping the 'typical' reader in mind.
- Structuring a world of varied, but minor characters.
- Keeping a running 'dossier' of details on each character.
- Mapping the locations.
- Answering 'fan' email addressed to the characters (you can answer as the character).
- Not becoming stale e.g., necessary to concentrate on a different minor character in each story, as well as the major one.
- Deciding on a fiction or non-fiction series or on the format of the stories.
- Characters can become 'legal properties' and being wary of how they are used.

Examples of book series

1. *The Gang O Kids* were set against an orienteering background. Orienteers belong to clubs and run weekly in both city and country areas. This sport requires participants to notice controls and to 'read' the features. By making the sleuths in the 8–12-year-old age group (two boys and two girls) they travelled with their parents but were relatively 'free' to roam. Books consisted of short stories where each 'mystery' was completed on one day at one location. Since many orienteering maps are created in old mining areas, realistic detail about nuggets, metal detectors, bushwalkers, elastic breaking in O-pants, camping and trail bikes was included. The problem was technology dated some of the clues and today's children would use GPS. Or Google Maps.

2. *The Frequent Flyer Twins* **series:** An airport setting and the situation of Ums (Unaccompanied Minors) children who travel alone. Different airports permitted plots revolving around quarantine

and customs regulations. Because airports are places of 'hello and goodbye', there was a varied cast.

The 10-year-old sleuths were carefully chosen as Asian-Australian twins, with a boy and girl of different skills to appeal to male and female readers. Technical difficulties included feasible reasons for the plane being delayed. In addition, it was often a challenge to find a reason why the twins might be able to sleuth alone. Considerable research at real airports including Melbourne, Cairns and Singapore, gave an air of authenticity to the story. Originally in print and now in eBook series. Due to the pandemic, airport quarantine and security procedures changed rapidly and dated some plots.

However, not all series have a technological theme. Even if they do, the readers will continue to follow their favourites as long as the characters and plots engage them.

Exercises

1. Create a character which has a six-book life, and which could adapt easily for TV. Consider the 8–12-year-old age group readership. Is the character human? What setting/period will you use? What is your title? Is it the name of your character? If so, is it distinctive and easily said?
2. Create a hero with a challenge, possibly that of a 'quest' that can be varied across several landscapes or stories. Will each story be self-contained, or must they read in sequence? For continuity, map the landscape of your story. If you invent words or concept, make sure you are consistent.

Checklist

1. Do you browse through bookshops and libraries?

2. Do you read reviews and note the publishers?

3. Do you Google or use your local library's reference sections?

4. What are some 'hot' topics for 3–5-year-olds? 6–8-year-olds? 8–12-year-olds?

5. Do you read children's review sites?

6. Have you attended authors' readings and launches?

7. Have you read translated children's books from other countries?

8. Have you joined a writers' organisations for the formal and informal marketing information?

9. Have you considered unusual angles on current events for non-fiction article topics as well as for book proposals?

CHAPTER 4

Genres

Definitions

Genre is the collective term given to a group of like-minded fiction. The term *genre* is a useful label to group stories fitting a certain convention. Genre writing may include:

- Romance
- Mystery
- Adventure
- Horror
- High fantasy
- Science fiction
- Historical fiction
- Magic realism.

Many 'serious writers' denigrate genre writing. Few have tried it. Genre writing follows a formula: Length, subject matter and conventions are established. Trying to craft a story within these limitations is a challenge. However, many writers successfully use these conventions as a framework upon which to hang an original story.

Sometimes a story will cross genres, so historical and romance, horror and mystery, horror and humour, high fantasy and thriller, high fantasy and adventure come into existence. Occasionally an author will deliberately or inadvertently create a new genre e.g., eco-fiction and thriller and adventure or historical fiction and mystery.

Differing kinds of genres

Style refers to the way something is written. It is the writer's personality coming out in the choice and arrangement of words.

Humour is a way of writing about a subject, rather than a genre. This could change. If sufficient numbers are published of a particular way of writing, it becomes a new genre. Possible genres may include:

- Spiritual
- Meditation
- Crystals
- Horoscopes
- Humour.

Subject matter is the topic which is chosen: e.g., horse stories.

Genre conventions are elements integral to the story, such as character types, key events, settings that's commonly found in a specific genre. The following is a general list of genre conventions.

Mystery:
- Crime case
- A detective
- Suspects
- Suspense
- Clues and red herrings
- No coincidences
- A solution.

Horror:
- Suspense/fear/violence
- Action
- Bizarre events
- Antagonist or phenomena
- Supernatural occurrences
- Naive character.

Fantasy:
- Other worlds
- A quest
- Internal logic
- Characters of different species.

Magic realism:
- The inexplicable occurs
- No explanation is necessary
- Reader suspends disbelief.

High fantasy:
- Complex other worlds
- A motive, or moral purpose
- A quest
- Unique protagonist
- Medieval timeline
- Ornate language.

Science fiction:
- Technologically based
- Scientifically plausible
- Future orientated.

Romance:
- Character in need of a partner
- Great deal of emotion and feeling
- Wish fulfilment
- Happy endings with couple reunited
- Sensitive male character
- Independent female character.

Adventure:
- Main character faces physical danger in a challenging setting
- Triumphant confrontation with villain
- Shows leadership and physical courage.

Writing romance

Romantic fiction is based on a belief in the universal importance of the subject of love. While most 'literary' novels published in this country might be lucky to sell 3000 copies, some authors of romantic fiction have been known to make a considerable income.

However, if you are writing a teenage romance, certain factors are important.

Planning

The basic framework is the initial attraction between the hero and the heroine (or same-sex protagonists) and the hurdling of obstacles that get in their way. Keep the plot simple; the important action is in the heads and hearts of the protagonists.

Ideally, the opening should introduce the settings, the hero/heroine, the romantic element and some conflict. Above all, it must capture the reader's attention as quickly as possible.

Setting

Why not use a familiar place to extend your plot? Here's how a heroine's surroundings are used to reflect their depressed mood:

> *So the next day, when I (Holly) needed a break from school, I caught a tram to South Beach then headed south on foot. The day was cold but still, the sky overcast, the sea a cold steel grey. Seagulls wheeled above my head and then, angry at being disturbed, flew off into the horizon. Strolling along, I watched tiny waves touch the shore then fade away into nothing.*

Plot

The story's main thrust is the development of the emotions of the characters. While there is always a certain antagonism between the characters, we must be aware of their sexual attraction for each other. You may need an ancillary theme to make your piece more interesting. When one budding writer tried to concentrate wholly on the romantic element of a working holiday, their readers wanted to know more about the job.

Characters

Severely limit cast to the two main characters and one or two others. In teenage romantic novels the protagonist often has a best friend. You must know your characters almost as well as you know yourself. Before beginning, name them: their names will give you some idea of the kind of people they are. Then have them fill out job application forms. Remember that they have a past. A good way to show it is through dialogue. Your characters need motives to explain their actions and these have to be related to their personalities.

Viewpoint

Teenage romances are often in first person. An interior monologue will show what the character is thinking, engage the reader's sympathy and add tension to the plot. Writing must be pacy, exciting and dramatic enough to make the characters strong. It isn't enough for one to fall in love with the other, the reader must as well.

Part of what makes these books romantic is the intensity of the language. Your writing should be emotional, yet simple and accurate. Avoid cliches and too many adjectives and adverbs. Show the reader what is happening rather than tell. Romantic fiction doesn't have to be second rate or purple prose. Many readers enjoy being enthralled by romantic daydreams at the same time as their intelligence tells them that much of this is fantasy.

Exercise

This exercise can be done in pairs or alone.

Potential readers: 8 to 10-year-olds.

Characters: Two 11-year-olds and one adult.

Location: A fast food outlet.

Problem: The characters are looking for a lost item.

1. Briefly outline the plot as if this was a mystery.
2. Write the first paragraph.
3. Now rewrite this paragraph as if this story was a horror.
4. Rewrite as science fiction.
5. Rewrite as a historical happening. This should give plenty of opportunity to write from a unique point of view, such as an 18th century tavern keeper, a cave person's barbecue or an ancient Egyptian street peddler.
6. How about fantasy? Good fantasy involves the real with the surreal. Show an unusual way of looking at the world.
7. High fantasy is very specialised and has conventions of its own. If you feel brave enough, try writing the opening paragraph in this mode.
8. Is there a possibility of romance? Something idealised?

NB. Possibly your characters maybe not be people as we know them. What's lost may not be considered valuable in our society.

Checklist

1. Does your story fit an existing genre?

---

2. In what way will this help in describing the story briefly?

---

3. Have you followed the conventions of length for this genre?

_____

_____

4. Is the title in keeping with the genre?

_____

_____

5. Read several titles from each genre. Identify the conventions.

_____

_____

_____

_____

6. List five possible considerations in writing a series.

_____

_____

_____

_____

CHAPTER 5

Business plans

Attitude: Amateur or professional

The amateur waits for things to happen, works for pure enjoyment or impulsively. The professional plans.

Initiate projects rather than just react to other people's invitations. A professional will plan the appropriate balance of projects for the next year e.g., a balance of fiction, non-fiction, short and long projects, solo and collaborative work, local and international speaking engagements, conferences, and a selection of speculative projects.

Establish a timetable

Establish realistic working hours. Writers don't necessarily work 9–5. Capitalise on the times you know you are most productive. Working alone, there is a danger of not knowing if you're not working enough or working too much. Energy, time and income management are important. Know roughly how much you need to earn per hour and how many chargeable hours a project will take. There needs to be a balance of commissioned and speculative work.

Projected income

Down-to-earth or fanciful? Certain work is easier to limit and to cost e.g., writing non-fiction. Fiction is time and energy consuming. Much depends on the speed and quality of ideas rather than the physical keyboard time.

If required to cost a writing project, add a 10% contingency payment to cover meanderings and mistakes.

Have a 'fall back' income or don't give up your day job. If someone is writing full-time, it's wise to have the equivalent of 3 days' worth of bread-and-butter income. Hundreds-and-thousands come later. Avoid having two fluctuating incomes in one household. When starting out, plan to have sufficient funds in hand to pay living and business expenses for a year.

Work and payment may be months apart. An advance on royalties may be paid on the signing of a contract and a further advance on the completion of the MS. However, these are advances against future royalties and must be earned from sales which may not occur for another year.

Alternatively, you can write on a 'fee for service' basis. This means a larger amount of money perhaps based on an hourly rate but no continuing interest if the project does well financially. Also, no subsidiary fees if the concept goes into other mediums. Even if the project doesn't do well, payment is already made.

The riskiest projects are those 'written on spec' (speculation) where there is no commitment by a publisher and the writer carries all the financial and emotional risk. Writing on spec may be appropriate until you have established a reputation. But to continue doing so will be financially detrimental.

General stages of writing as a career

1. **Writing with no particular publisher in mind.**
2. **Canvassing for expressions of interest** before investing too much time and energy: e.g., a publisher says 'Yes, we could be interested in a subject like that for our list when you have finished, but it would have to fit our format.' This does not bind a publisher to any financial support. An expression of interest is not a contract, but it's a start.
3. **Negotiating contracts:** A financial and a legal commitment in terms of a contract and fee before going beyond a synopsis and sample chapter.

Handling different projects

Vary the length and financial return of projects to maintain some cash flow. Otherwise, a yearly royalty may be the sole income. A combination of copy writing, speaking engagements, judging literary competitions, taking creative writing workshops, participating in 'writer-in-residency' programs and permissions fees for using original work in other formats is recommended.

Keep an open mind

Be prepared to do unexpected jobs, like scripting for a stand-up comic or editing a kids' magazine. Although a creator may be perceived as someone who only writes fiction or who never tackles picture story books, it is often the least expected project that proves to be the financial or artistic winner. Be wary of commissioned work that removes any royalty payment. Keep the rights to fees such as PLR (public lending right). And never sign away electronic or subsidiary rights.

Observe the opposition

Learn from competitors in allied fields. Don't plagiarise but be aware of what other creators are working on. By staying informed about the work of others and recognising emerging trends, authors can maintain relevance and find new avenues for creative inspiration in the ever-evolving world of writing and publishing.

Use the Internet

Use Google to your advantage. There is a constant flow of information about writers' networks, literary markets, and specifically blogs about writing children's books. Additionally, consider joining online forums, social media groups, and participating in webinars or virtual writing conferences to tap into the collective wisdom of the writing community and stay updated on the latest insights and opportunities in the field.

Handling stress

For some creators, stress is a sense of pressure or continual tension coupled with a feeling of compulsion. Others call this distress and regard stress as a stimulant. Stress can result from:

- Extreme physical exertion
- Prolonged mental demands
- Many deadlines
- Dislike of the work ahead
- Domestic strains
- Overload
- Unexpected illness or accident.

Learn to take time off. Feel in charge of the business, rather than letting the business take charge. Pacing is important. Learn to catnap. Talk out problems with other writers or friends. Have contingency plans for deadlines and a colleague with comparable skills who can fill in for you in an emergency. However, realise that some people need an external deadline to get them going.

Relevant business services

Consider whether you need a:

- Tax agent or accountant
- Computer accounting program
- A company structure
- Letter of agreement between collaborators
- Literary agent
- Speakers' agency to handle bookings
- Publicist for your corporate image as an author
- Your own website with online bookstore
- Membership of professional organisations to access their support.

Now, can you afford these services? Which are the more strategic for you at this stage of your writing career?

Take time to discern if you have enough budget to afford any of these services. Reflect and decide which should take priority and which are more strategic for you at this stage of your writing career.

Business basics

When you are setting up a business, consider:

- Cash flow and income projection for one year
- Basic equipment: computer, Internet connection, printer, etc
- Headed stationery, business cards, book marks, etc
- Copying, casual research help, couriers
- Postage, paper, envelopes and printer ink
- Equipment maintenance contract
- Courses or conference fees to update skills.

Networking

A network is a group with equal but different skills working in similar fields. Age or gender doesn't matter.

Networking is crucial for authors for several reasons. First, it helps authors establish connections with publishers, literary agents, and other industry professionals who can provide opportunities and guidance. Second, networking allows authors to engage with fellow writers, sharing experiences and knowledge that can enhance their craft. Third, it aids in building an audience and readership through social media and author events.

Overall, networking is a vital tool for gaining visibility, support and access in the competitive world of publishing. Networks don't work if the flow is one way: it must be between equals.

Hints

1. Keep working at the end of your week until the major items on the 'to-do' list are finished.
2. Work to an external deadline: e.g., appointment with a collaborator.
3. Use email to send completed work at hours convenient to you.
4. Encourage family and friends to see a writer as 'at work' even if still in the family home. A writer's attitude will determine others.

Exercises

1. Estimate weekly cash-flow. Draw up a projection for the next 6 months under the following headings:
   a. Opening balance
   b. Anticipated receipts/income
   c. Expenses
   d. Closing balance

2. Keep a record of time management for several days:

7.00–7.30am:	Got up, had breakfast, showered.
7.30–8.00am:	Checked hardcopy of non-fiction piece.
8.00–8.30am:	Dropped children at school.
8.30–10.00am:	Worked on short fiction for X magazine.
11.am–noon:	Zoom meeting re possible film project. Exercise.
3.30pm:	Pick up kids.
8pm–10pm:	Administrivia re writing. Accounts. Queries.

   Add up the time directly relevant to income-earning projects.

   Plan tomorrow, so the time is spent more productively. (Realistically, make one improvement!)

Checklist

1. Do you see yourself as an amateur or a professional?
   _____
   _____

2. Have you drawn up a realistic timetable?
   _____
   _____

3. Projected income: is this optimistic or realistic?

4. Do you maintain files on income and expenses?

5. Are you open to other writing opportunities?

6. Are you monitoring your opposition?

7. How do you cope with stress?

8. Have you accessed online sites relevant to your projects?

9. What expertise (people or skills) might you need for your business in the next three months?

CHAPTER 6

Overcoming procrastination

Don't start at chapter 1

A book does not have to be written sequentially. Very often the original Chapter 1 will be scrapped in favour of a more relevant version in the light of the rest of the story. A working title, chapter headings and sequence may change several times. Remember, until a book is published, nothing is permanent.

Commit to a deadline

This is where having a co-writer is a useful discipline: one will insist on the other working. Have a private deadline ahead of the official one. Use spare time for extra editing. Avoid scheduling simultaneous deadlines and/or periods of personal stress.

Estimating the time to write fiction from original idea, or innovative format to edited copy, is hard. Non-fiction is generally easier to assess in terms of query letters, interview times, research, checking with expert readers and writing.

Switch between projects

Vary the type of work: research, interviewing, writing first drafts, rewriting and editing other drafts, and administrivia. Have a mixture of projects, some solitary, some collaborative. When low, research and refuel the imagination. A large project can be overpowering. Take one step at a time.

Keeping relaxed

Maintaining a state of relaxation is not just about reducing stress; it's also a valuable aspect of the creative process for authors. By regularly practicing relaxation techniques, like meditation or simply taking a leisurely walk, authors create a mental space that allows their minds to wander freely. This state of mental freedom can lead to serendipitous moments in writing, where unexpected plots, characters or ideas emerge organically. These happy accidents can infuse a story with authenticity and novelty, often surprising the author as much as the reader. Embracing this sense of serendipity and allowing the unconscious mind to take over can result in more vibrant and imaginative storytelling, adding depth and richness to the narrative. So, don't underestimate the power of relaxation in nurturing creativity and unlocking the untapped potential of your storytelling abilities.

Writer-in-residency

Published authors are sometimes invited to become writers-in-residence. This can be an additional source of income, an opportunity to analyse techniques, and a welcome change of occupation when the writing isn't going well. But occasionally there is a 'downside.'

'Few authors are psychologically equipped to be a writer-in-residency,' says author Garry Disher. 'Temperamentally, a writer needs to be diplomatic, highly energetic, adaptable to a range of people, technically proficient and able to teach.'

Disher, the versatile author of award-winning children's books and adult literature is realistic about the demands placed on introspective writers and suggests that 'in-residence' appointments are 'hard work' and not an expense paid, exotic holiday jaunt. Other authors agree but stress the benefits of demonstrating techniques with hopeful writers who need help in expressing their ideas.

How does a residency work?

Schools, libraries or service groups host an author to provide a focus for a festival, conference, workshop or camp. Their aim is to inspire locals and give easy access to specialist techniques and different ways of thinking.

The term 'in-residence' can have several meanings. Sometimes an author is attached to an institution for several weeks, 'stays' in a single location or moves rapidly with a 'minder' to visit far flung groups in remote areas. Or it may mean being given space to work, financial support and the chance to create in return for talks and comments on the manuscripts of local writers.

Much depends upon the organiser, the program aims and the funding available. Costs such as fees, accommodation and travel are often split between the locals and Arts Council subsidies.

Funding bodies tend to favour submissions from isolated communities. Often an entrepreneurial organiser arranges for an author to 'make something happen' locally. Other 'residencies' are attached to innovative institutions that aim to provide enriching programs for students.

Garry Disher has been writer-in-the-community for the TasWriters and the State Library of Queensland and was involved in a program that included talks in eight prisons. He said 'In future, I'll only work in a TAFE or a university with small groups of hand-picked people. There are benefits for the community in 'whistle-stop' performances, but not for the writer.'

Occasionally a writer is treated as a relief teacher in some schools and not even formally introduced to students. In other regions, hospitality is thoughtful, and the audiences are well-prepared with access to the writer's works.

A weekend residential camp offers different opportunities. Krista Bell, a broadcaster, reviewer and author, ran live-in, book-orientated events for year 8 students. Authors-in-residence at these Virtuoso Weekends have included authors Margaret Clark, John Marsden and illustrator Terry Denton.

'Formal sessions alternate with casual opportunities to talk with the resident authors about their writing secrets,' she says. 'The chance to talk informally, especially for shy, beginning young writers is very important.'

Authors praise organisers who ensure books are publicised beforehand, making discussions more meaningful.

Exercises

1. Take a certain word and find a word for each letter.

   For example: use the word 'sport'.

   Strength
   Powerball
   Organisation
   Routine
   Trail

   Use these to make up a plot. Here are some other words you might use:

   FANTASY, ADVENTURE, ROMANCE, MYSTERY, SCIENCE.

2. Take a long walk. Listen to music. Don't concentrate on the problem. Just let your mind rove.

3. Read. Often what someone else has written will trigger ideas.

Checklist

1. Start writing.
2. Keep an open mind.
3. Practise relaxing.
4. Commit to a deadline.
5. Collaborate.
6. Start anywhere, not necessarily at the beginning.
7. Run simultaneous projects and switch between them.

CHAPTER 7

Working with multimedia

Definitions

Today it's likely that musicians, photographers, lyricists, illustrators, animators, programmers AND writers will be involved in the one project, regardless of the term used for the format.

Multimedia has multiple meanings, depending upon the background of the speaker. Confusion arises as to whether people are speaking of the ideas content or the format in which it is presented. Format names like CD or disk have been superseded and today's label will be dated soon.

Tech-savvy people claim 'multimedia' came out of the computer world and is when sound and movement are added to a program and there is user interaction. They claim that 'multimedia' relates only to what can be performed on a computer screen.

Others disagree. 'Multi' means many. And as long as more than two media formats are used, they claim it can be called 'multimedia'. A cartoonist-illustrator said that *'multimedia relates to the format not the content.'* If one of his magazine cartoons is taken into other formats, with sound and movement, the cartoon's satirical ideas content will be the same, but the format will have been changed into multimedia.

Some claim that if a book is adapted for stage or TV, it is NOT multimedia, it is only an adaptation because there is no obvious user-interaction.

However, if the story from the original novel is adapted for stage and for film with accompanying music, then it could be argued that it fits under multimedia, because it's available in more than two formats.

Unless one is multi-talented as author, illustrator, designer, computer programmer, art director and producer, the writer will need to work as part of a team. Some writers enjoy the stimulation of working as part of a creative team with the challenge of budgets and deadlines. Others find that the more technically complex the project becomes, and the more contributors involved, the greater the personal stress. Others thrive on risk as stimulation.

Although some may prefer to 'author' novels or short stories in isolation rather than 'author' computer games or animation, it is important that writers be aware of the innovative formats in which those ideas and plots may be expressed.

Important things to keep in mind about working in multimedia:

- Be prepared to experiment.
- Pick reputable but skilled colleagues.
- Do your homework. Study the medium and the methods of the people you will work with. Look at their track record. Do they just talk or do they actually get projects up?
- Don't be taken in by titles or the size of the temporary office.
- If the business card says … 'and associates' it's probably a one person band.
- Be wary of unproductive meetings, vague promises but no contracts, late or missing advances or unrealistic deadlines.
- Distrust over-enthusiasm and effusiveness.
- If you keep phoning back, but no one's there. Warning!

Media changes so fast, that these examples will be out of date next week. So will the language for the labels. However, attitudes towards being willing to risk experimenting in new formats is a constant.

Practitioners' responses

What trends have you noticed in the field?

'It's safest to stay six months behind the cutting edge and never buy first version software. Keep a watchful eye on the latest "gadget" but remain silent until the majority picks it up.'

To what extent is there a danger of investing a lot of time and energy in areas which may be quickly superseded?

'The only experimental areas that I get into are for artistic purposes. The technology moves so fast that it is inevitable that it will be superseded or obsolete within five years.'

Developing children's games

A specialist area, these games are created by teams including authors, designers, software engineers and development managers. Rarely would an inexperienced writer be invited to join an established software company. Opportunities may arise for adapting original publications such as developing adventure stories games or perhaps collaborating with a freelance software designer who aims to sell the game to a larger company.

Some risk capital or working for deferred returns may be required to 'get the project up' in an innovative area such as picture book apps. Interestingly, major software-design-breakthroughs – originate in work done for children. The instructions need to be simple, but the possible variations need to be abundant to continue to interest children's imagination. Computer programmers like to design controlled environments where the users are fairly predictable. Imaginative, young children like to experiment. This is an extra challenge for the designers of children's games.

One designer suggests:

- Make software flexible: children can learn by exploring but it also it fits a wider age range.
- Users are demanding more interactivity and unpredictability in their games but avoid violence.

- Since adults choose the child's software, parents and grandparents like to justify the expense by being able to say it's 'educational'.
- Provide opportunities for adult and child to interact together. The child should also be able to have fun without adult supervision.

Working in animation

A production house will commission the writer and the designated animator within an agreed budget and on a specific topic, usually as part of a series. Or the writer will originate the concept and work with an animator through several drafts of a script. Some animators are also writers, and versatility makes a writer potentially more employable. It's likely that the writer will have to create character outlines as well as a synopsis.

If the animation (cartoon) is for very young children and likely to be sold internationally, there will probably be a voice-over which can be dubbed easily into another language. Subtitles in any language are useless for non-reading children. So scripts need to show, not tell.

> The intrinsic nature of quality animation is labour-intensive, with even a short cartoon requiring literally thousands of sequences drawings (and/or computer generated images.)
>
> Animation is often used in TV advertising and to illustrate sensitive subjects. Animation is seen as a sort of embarrassment buffer for sensitive areas. Cartoon characters have an innocent quality. Animation is a field of unlimited potential. It is a very suitable vehicle to get across a vision of the future and show things which haven't happened yet. – *Anonymous animator*

The high cost of experimentation means that individual, original projects are unlikely to be funded unless they have mass market international appeal. A 'series' character or theme or a proven 'classic' adapted from other media is more likely to justify the expense of digital development.

Dual language education is growing where parents buy the apps, so their child learns a second language, but with the assistance of movement, music, interactive responses and fun.

Parents or schools need the appropriate hardware, and this can be a cost limitation.

Creating an author website

Q. Why did you want a website?

Answer: To save time. I receive many letters from children who ask about plot, favourite foods or where I write. An author web page provides the basic book information, a bio and a hi-res author PR photo for downloading. My aim was to write the information once. I have always written individual answers. But the administrivia was becoming overwhelming.

The second reason is for publicity. A website is the international shopfront for a creator.

The third reason was to keep in tune with my readers. Children are at ease with digital access. They see it as the natural way to gather information.

Q. How important is it for an author to keep up to date technologically?

Authors who are not online are missing out. The speed at which information travels, means that unless you are accessible, you'll be left out of proposed projects.

Q. How do you actually prepare material to go online?

Web writing needs to be shorter with emphasis on visuals. Book covers can be scanned. Relevant book illustrations can be shown. 'Short' paragraphs. Question and answer format. Once I grasped that the material is non-linear and often hidden behind a key term or picture, creating titles and subheadings became even more important.

Q. Do all authors need to be electronically available?

Yes. Being an author is also about marketing ideas. Authors need to be electronically available. A website is merely a tool, the quality of the ideas content still matters.

Edutainment

Electronic entertainment with an educational aim is supposed to teach the child content or process. Good structuring and relevant material ensure faster learning. Responsible adults feel comforted by the notion that their child is doing something useful instead of 'just playing'.

Ironically, since playing involves 'trial and error', the child, like the adult often learns electronic processes by just messing around. Edutainment often implies non-violent material, which is also attractive.

For example, most adults would prefer a child to learn hand-eye co-ordination and navigation skills on a 'Quest for the Sunken Treasure' program, rather than a 'Kill the Baddies' program where progress is determined by how many 'baddies' are killed by a variety of weapons.

A game designer needs to balance challenge with ability, taking into account the age and intellectual skills of the players. An edutainment script needs to fit within the educational philosophy of the client.

Children's TV

Children's TV is one of the most common sources of media that children use for information and enjoyment. Channel 7's Consultant on Children's Television, says '... *regulatory framework protects locally made TV commercial broadcasters are required by law to air children's and pre-schoolder programs specifically for Australian children and pre-schoolers.*'

So, a potential scriptwriter needs to be aware of the current regulations governing the content of children's programs. Most practitioners have a working knowledge of restrictions relating to language, subjects or audience age and program length but these regulations change quickly, so it's wise to contact authorities such as the Australian Children's Television Foundation.

Adaptation proposals: Picture book to stage production

Popularity in one medium will not necessarily translate into another as the age group and attention span may be different. However, if the character has universal emotional appeal, chances increase.

This is an example of a concept originally presented as a 32-page picture story book, *Stickybeak* but was then adapted for the children's theatre stage. Following is the extended concept in the format in which it was presented to prospective theatre producers. Note the subheadings which make it easier for a busy producer to pick up the major aspects.

Proposal: Stickybeak – Director Duck

A play for 3–7-year-olds.
By Christine Anketell and Hazel Edwards

The book

The duck character from Hazel Edwards' *Stickybeak* (Penguin) has proved immensely popular indicated by sales in Australasia and overseas in the USA, Canada, UK and China. The popularity of this character is confirmed by awards, television readings and the consistent fan mail but also the letters and pictures addressed specifically to Stickybeak. The majority are prep to grade 3 children.

The character

Stickybeak's appeal lies in his exuberant personality. Like a 4-year-old child, he leaps to action without regard for consequences, speaks before he thinks and has a joyful disregard of the social niceties. These endearing attributes result in Stickybeak finding himself in hilarious situations with which children identify. They recognise that he is one of them.

Target audience

We envisage a theatre piece for the 3–7-year-olds that revolves around the character of Stickybeak. Puppetry, mask and mime linked by commedia style visual humour, will bring to life this character while exploring the themes of friendship, responsibility and self-esteem, which are pertinent issues for this age group.

Themes

A children's farm was chosen as the setting for this play. Hence the production could be done outdoors i.e., the zoo, Collingwood children's farm. The production would work equally as well by incorporating this concept into the set design for touring to schools and kindergartens.

The theme of having to cope with an unfamiliar surrounding by drawing on personal resources is relevant for children entering school or kindergarten.

Stickybeak's response to his new situation will alleviate some anxieties although a few of his solutions are humorously inappropriate. By establishing Stickybeak as a director we are introducing children to theatre practice and subsequent disciplines.

Cast

3–4 puppeteer/actors depending upon whether the music is live or pre-recorded and operated by the tour manager.

Synopsis: (This was provided in a one-page outline).

How not to write for the latest medium

1. Which medium *is* the latest? Some formats will be superseded within months.
2. Spend only a proportion of working time in the risky area of new technology unless someone else is paying the bills. Risk management for writers is vital.
3. Be wary. Although some scripting skills are transferable, and being known to have had experience even in a short-lived technology is beneficial to other projects, one can get 'caught'.
4. Avoid techno-playing and not keeping an eye on income-earning work e.g., acquiring computer-ese rather than writing. Some play with the equipment, exchange programs, talk about the value of the latest 'toy' but never get to write anything. Ration your time, at least 80% to be income-earning.
5. Some experimental media require expensive hardware which is likely to date quickly. Software can also be superseded. Individuals may not be able to afford or have access to hi-tech unless working in an umbrella organisation. Since the educational market is an important segment for children's writers, be aware that schools can't all afford to buy or lease the latest equipment.
6. A compromise may be to adapt existing stories from an 'older' format (i.e. a book) into the new technology. If you control the copyright, there are less likely to be legal problems with gaining permissions.

7. Intellectual property becomes an important issue as material is likely to go immediately into an electronic world market. So it may be feasible to spend a long time on a high quality product for a bigger more immediate market, but only if there's some control over sales.

8. Instant copying can be a problem in all media, and the originator may not gain a fair share.

9. Working with professionals from other fields such as computer graphics, is part of your professional 'keeping up to date'. If the writer offers the story content, and the company trades the technical skills, it's an equal exchange.

10. Children welcome the latest technology as the norm. While adults writing for children may need to unlearn techniques suited to older formats, the child audience is receptive to innovative combinations of idea and format.

Exercises

Remember that to fit multimedia format, it needs to be interactive i.e., using audio, visuals and offer choices.

1. **'Cool' journeys**

    A concept for a time-travel animation with a central character called 'the Explorer' aimed at 8–12-year-old audience. Indicate the specific 'cool' journeys e.g., Antarctic, Mars, Into the Refrigerator. What aspects of user/interaction will you suggest so that the Viewer can make choices in the plot?

    The animation may take the form of a cartoon or be included in a digital device. Outline your concept on one page under subheadings such as

    - Title
    - Concept and length
    - Audience and their needs
    - Cast
    - Settings
    - Conflicts
    - Number of stories
    - Choices
    - Outcomes
    - Prospective market

2. **Bird in the hand!**

    In 10 lines evoke a bird character with catchy name which could be appropriate for varied media and eventual merchandising.ie a soft toy, t-shirts, mugs etc. Consider possible adventures with choices in the plot for an 8-year-old child to click onto.

3. **S.A.L.T.**

    A digital production house has approached you as they have funding available for an educational multimedia project about S.A.L.T. By 9 AM tomorrow they want you to email them 3 or 4 ideas of the ways in which you might tackle this concept. You meet the deadline and fulfil the brief.

Checklist

1. A definition of the term multimedia can include:

   _____

   _____

2. Name several skills that might be useful to a multimedia practitioner?

   _____

   _____

3. There are several reasons why it might pay an author to set up an author webpage. These include:

   _____

   _____

   _____

4. Edutainment is a generic term which covers:

   _____

   _____

5. Working in multimedia contains some traps for the unwary. These can include:

   _____

   _____

6. It is important for all creators to understand the latest medium innovations because:

   _____

   _____

   _____

CHAPTER 8

Commercial scripting

Fostering interactivity with commercial scripting

Commercial scripting may involve:

1. A paying audience of children and/or adults.
2. Staying within a precise brief about staging time and budget which will control numbers of scenes and cast size.
3. Exploiting familiarity e.g., adaptations of classics which will mean a far wider audience: *The Hobbit*.
4. Utilising unusual or outdoor settings by dramatising well-known stories on location e.g., *Charlotte's Web* in a children's farm, *Peter Pan* in the Botanic Gardens.
5. Providing a story to dramatise a digital game.
6. Using puppetry and mime to encourage interaction.

Script writers enjoy the faster and tighter characterisation in dialogue. They enjoy the additional input from actor, director, dramaturg and the ambience of the stage.

Some novelists invited to script their books dislike the feeling of losing control of their story. Other creators feel reassured by the input of others; but only if it's high quality.

Scripting for children where the actors are adult professionals differs from writing scripts for students to perform in class. Differences between these include:

1. Cast size
2. Complexity of plot
3. Language difficulty
4. Emotional range
5. Technical intricacies (e.g., sound, lighting, props, etc).

In addition to dialogue, sound effects (SFX) music, actors' appearances, scenery and props, and even the audiences' own reactions, can all become part of the performance.

Student-performed scripts may include those to be televised, sound recorded, staged or those meant for class use. The emphasis is upon participation rather than providing an entertainment for the audience.

TV scripting

Television scripting is collaborative work. A television company may provide the story outline and existing characters within a series. Often the plot has been storyboarded and a story editor will have considerable input. Other constraints can include:

- Number of indoor and outdoor scenes (external are more expensive)
- Number of available actors
- Script and/or performance time
- Cliff-hangers of tension prior to commercial breaks.

Initially, it is highly unlikely that a newcomer will be asked to originate a commercial one-hour TV script. Most writers for TV serve an apprenticeship writing for existing 'soapies' which are aimed at the adult market but are often adolescent oriented.

Organisations like The Australian Children's Television Foundation have successfully funded and internationally promoted quality children's programs. They invite creators from other media for specific projects.

New writers are given opportunities to learn techniques of:

- Scene break-down
- Storyboarding

- Characterisation
- Budgeting
- Time-management
- Critique
- Multiple rewrites.

New writers are paid at a lower rate, but again this is part of the apprenticeship. Experience is measured in half hour credits as well as the quality of the production. Through the learning process, they will learn to cope with the disappointment of a paid project that eventually doesn't get aired on TV.

On application, most TV and children's entertainment companies will list their current requirements for new writers breaking into the television field. Sample layouts of current series can be bought so that proposals by new writers can be presented in the acceptable format. These formats change from company to company, so check up-to-date information. Realistically, opportunities come by word of mouth. So, have writing samples prepared. Also, complete half-hour sample scripts of original material – or material based on existing series – to use as samples of writing ability. Don't expect these to be performed. They are ads for your skills.

FAQs of TV scripting

1. Where are independent TV production companies listed?

Check the current script writers' professional organisations which keep data on relevant markets, projects, subsidies and opportunities for writers.

2. Is it better to approach an independent producer or a large company?

Depends on the type of project proposed. An independent producer may take a personal interest in an unusual project and push it. Or a director may pitch it to a producer who must organise the financial support. Regular channels and a big company are a better bet for a mainstream project. Budgets, types of funding available and the ability to write appropriate submissions affect whether your project has a chance of interesting a producer.

3. How long should it take to write a one-hour script?

Roughly, a page per minute is a guide. This is a minute of performance time, not the time it takes to write. A commercial one-hour script may be less than 60 minutes because of commercial breaks.

4. What's the going rate for an hour's TV script?

There are payments for different stages. Payment is often related to signing of contract, then first draft, second draft stages.

5. What are residuals?

Additional fees paid to those involved in the project once the TV program is sold again.

6. On average, how long does it take to break into the market?

It depends on how determined you are. A 5-year apprenticeship is average. Variables such as luck, talent, timing, and topicality of script submissions will affect the outcome. Who you know helps, but only if you have the skills.

Other digital formats

Although the screen size may be the same, the purpose in scripting for online rather than TV may be different. Some children's entertainment is just recycled TV or film. Whereas, instructional or training programs are aimed at imparting skills: e.g., how not to get lost in the bush, pet-training for owners, vegetarian cooking for Year 7 camps.

Scripting facts for educational packages or online is usually commissioned and is a good area for teachers to break in. With webcams or even mobile phone filming being accessible these days, 'freebie' amateur scripting for community organisations is a good place to start.

Scripting for film

Writing a film script is financially risky. Scripts must be a minimum of 90 minutes and tend to be 'one-offs'. Director-writers are common and only the persistent producers manage to raise film money, often after years of planning. Even if the film is made, this doesn't guarantee that it will be screened on a commercial circuit. Interest is often concentrated in the scripting of classics or film adaptations of popular novels with themes that will attract both an adult and Young Adult audience.

Most film scripts don't get up despite passionate creators. However, if made, children's films have a longer life internationally, and with new audiences growing every five years. Choice of subject matter of continuing interest is crucial. Or maybe the style in which it is produced becomes highly valued. Awards help extend the life of the film.

Scripting for puppet plays

Writing a puppet script can be highly adventurous. Some productions tour kindergartens and schools while others are theatre-based or 'street theatre'.

In puppet plays:

- Characters can be people or things e.g., a flying doona.
- Settings are limited only by imagination.
- Roles are limited by the number of puppeteers although it's possible for 'doubling up' or one player manipulating more than one character.
- A range of possible puppets exist from finger, glove or sock puppets to giant puppets where the actors wear a costume and their bodies become one with the puppet.
- Some touring commercial puppet companies are versatile two-handers where the audio may be pre-recorded to enable two actors to present multiple characters. Scripts, songs and music may be original. Sets are easily 'bumped in'. When scripting, writers need to be aware of creating roles which fit small but skilled puppet casts.

Miming

Although there are no words used in a mime, the artist still needs a script. Often a mime artist will create personal performance scripts. These scripts serve as a blueprint for their non-verbal storytelling, helping the artist choreograph their movements and convey their intended messages with precision.

Unusual scripting

Have an open mind to explore different forms of scripting, as opportunities may arise. Consider the audience and consider the actor's needs: A ventriloquist who operated a doll in shopping malls needed a new humorous script. When written, too many m's and n's made it impossible for a ventriloquist to perform when the doll was talking simultaneously. The script had to be rewritten, minus m's and n's.

Or perhaps you might write a script for celebratory events, e.g., birthday party entertainers need more than just a string of jokes. Another idea could be birthday and celebration poems for performance. There may be instances of a less jubilant opportunities, such as writing a eulogy for a child's funeral. Scripting for stand-up performers is another growing area, although many write their own.

CHAPTER 9

Educational scripting

Classroom scripts

Typically, an educational publisher briefs a writer for a class performance script for junior secondary students. Versatile roles which can be played by male, female or diverse gendered students. Requirements include a cast of at least 10–25, a contemporary issue and running time within a 40-minute period.

Theatre in education

Sponsored scripts have tight budgets and strict briefs where the content is controlled. The audience is likely to be school based and the actors are required to tour. This means the props and sets need to be simple because they have to be moved often. It's called 'bumping in.' Theatre in education (TIE) is usually performed by young energetic and versatile actors who can generate their own material.

Often submissions need to be written at least a year ahead of production and likely sponsors e.g., health organisations, sport foundations, must be found. Sometimes controversial topics such as gender, bullying, land rights, sexual abuse are specifically commissioned to generate discussion. The audience is encouraged to participate as part of the performance either as a group character or 'Greek chorus'.

Rarely would speculative scripts be performed unless they coincidentally fitted the curriculum theme e.g., environment/climate change.

Scripting for audiobooks

Audio stories and plays have a consistent market, especially with personal listening devices. Increasingly, those exercising or travelling listen to audio stories. Also useful for encouraging literacy as words are pronounced correctly and can be imitated.

Advantages for writers include the relative simplicity of using sound effects and music instead of complicated scene changes and multiple props. Audio offers a multiplicity of voices and time-jump possibilities. Don't ignore the factual or documentary area. Children's audio for use in cars is increasing. Read alongs of favourite books are becoming more popular on digital devices. Even some children's hospitals like Westmead have their own 'BedRock' audio station which has to work hard to distract and entertain child patients.

Community radio stations are sometimes prepared to allow you to produce a children's program. Pay is minimal or non-existent, but the experience will hone your scripting. Reviewing books, children's literary events, presenter's links and interviews for radio still need scripting.

Performance lyrics, rap and poetry

Performers read, sing or perform poems written by others or by themselves. Rappers can energetically perform their own work with actions and music. They perform in festivals, street theatre, public television or radio, schools or even at birthday celebrations with personalised poems. Few poets make a living but many gain significant satisfaction from getting their poetry heard or published. Some self-publish and sell copies at their gigs, others find paying markets, sometimes in education or online. Stand-up comics are the growth area for scripting.

Shopping centres and street theatre

During holiday periods, shopping centre management often commission 'entertainment acts' to attract children and their 'shopping' parents to malls. In the past this was ad hoc, low-grade entertainment with a character in a hired suit relating to a product. Background noises and interruptions made it difficult for performers to do anything other than clown around.

However, demand has increased for more sophisticated scripting. Maybe the local council commissions a theme such as 'care for the environment' or 'our local history'. Some avant-garde ideas are introduced through these venues. These still need to be scripted, though often the performers create their own short skits. Challenging to perform but some writers love the experience.

Hints for scripting plays

1. Layout is important so actors can identify their dialogue from directions.
2. Distinguish between plays written for children to be performed by adult professional actors, and students performing for other children or a general audience. Choice of vocabulary, cast size, speech length and running time will differ. Often one role has a lot of reading e.g., storyteller or narrator. Indicate in the cast list that this role requires a good reader/actor.
3. Action or 'stage business' is needed. Characters need to do, not just talk.
4. An 'elastic' chorus means the extras will all have parts.
5. Roles aren't limited to 'people.' Why not have characters become bricks in a wall, flowers in a garden, abstractions such as 'virtues and vices' or one of the 'Seven Deadly Sins.'
6. Underlying conflict is vital but avoid fights or chasing around the stage. Conflict lies in the subject matter and can be between or within characters.
7. Structurally the easiest play format is a parody: A TV quiz program, folktale or a well-known 'soapie' is easily satirised. Much of the effectiveness would depend on the audience knowing the original. Update a well-known plot to another time or location.
8. Funny plays and TV scripts sell. Humour may come from the farcical situation or funny characters. Wordplay can be lost if badly spoken or timed, or if too much else is going on. If you enjoy 'punning', write for audio.

9. Sound test the script. Test the words when said aloud by an actor.
10. Establish differences quickly by what characters say and do. Choose names that are easy to say. Create gender neutral characters and varying ages. Don't overuse stuttering or swearing.
11. Limit set changes. In a 40-minute play, one setting is sufficient. Don't insist on elaborate costumes or props as this reduces the chances of performing your play.
12. Limit professional actors to four or the play will be uneconomic to produce. Suggest extra characters with mobile phone, sound effects, off-stage voices or someone that is talked about. If costumes, puppets or masks are interchangeable, this may give an illusion of more actors.
13. The play's running time varies from half to a minute a page, depending upon the ratio of action to dialogue and how often the audience laughs. A poor performance usually means the play will be shorter.
14. Allow audience participation. When playing to children, why not use them as an extra character like old-style pantomime 'goodies and baddies'.
15. A climax is needed at the play's end. The problem needs to be solved in a dramatic and yet emotionally satisfying way. A twist could be useful. The writer can use 'offstage' space where an actor enters or leaves through the audience. Music and sound effects can be used to create mood, as can silence. An actor may speak directly to the audience to get them on side.

Scripting for documentaries

Often used as an educative medium, factual plays involve both audience and players. The content is varied e.g., road safety, dental health, consent, bushfire preparation etc. However, it's best to avoid propaganda. Opportunities to discuss sensitive topics arise during rehearsals, performance, and after production.

Factual scripts need to be:

- Highly researched and fact checked
- Large enough to include all class members (up to 25)

- Flexible with choruses
- Humorous to sell the story
- Legally copiable
- Discussion starters.

Novelisations

If a film or TV series has been popular, a novelisation may be commissioned, but not always from the original script writer. Novelisation is more than joining up existing dialogue with a few descriptive paragraphs. It must work as a book in its own right, even for someone who has never seen the film. A film-still or photo will probably be used on the cover.

Fostering literacy with scripts

Practising reading a script so you can perform it for others, gives a 'sociable' reason for reading. So often a simple script can encourage literacy. But the subject matter needs to be relevant for the new reader e.g., teaching how to get a driver's licence for secondary school students. When scripts align with the reader's interests and real-life situations, they can become a powerful tool for developing essential literacy skills and practical knowledge.

Exercise

Here is an example of a 'didactic' (teaching) scenario. How would you develop this humorously as:

1. A classroom play?
2. A professional production?

Title: BUTTS

Issue: SMOKING

Setting: SMOKESVILLE HIGH.

Style: Heavy messages rarely work. *Satire* is useful device. If peer group pressure is the issue, smoking is merely the means through which it is shown. One of the challenges for a writer is that the negative character is always more interesting, so chances are that the BUTT's chorus will allow for personality-plus.

Possible characters and ideas:

If you're stuck, think along these lines.

Is the story set in the past or in the future? Use a character who transcends time e.g., Sir Walter Raleigh who discovered tobacco. Use these attributes to create a unique character. One idea is to focus on the story of how peer pressure is never a good idea and develop the story to see how it impacts the characters in the story.

Also note that both smoking and vaping irritate your airways and lungs, which can contribute to several health conditions affecting your lungs, including asthma and chronic bronchitis. Think of how you can script this. Trial your draft script with a group, receive feedback and then re-work it.

The title page of the MS could be set out like this:

> *Title:*
> *By:*
> *A classroom playscript for Junior Secondary Students.*
>
> *Running time:*   minutes.
> *Cast:*   Minimum number:
>   Maximum number:

Props:
Sound effects:
Setting:
Script:
Curriculum links:

Checklist

1. Commercial scripting possibilities may include writing for:

2. Educational scripting can include:

3. Points that distinguish between scripting commercially for a children's audience, and a children's classroom plays include:

4. How might reading scripts help literacy?

5. Any differences between scripting for TV and scripting for a film?

6. In a novelisation, what must be taken into account as well as the dialogue?

   _____

   _____

7. Some unusual opportunities for script writers are:

   _____

   _____

8. In educational scripting, why might an expandable chorus be a useful device?

   _____

   _____

9. Humour usually sells. Why?

   _____

   _____

   _____

CHAPTER 10

Crafting a story

Crafting an intriguing plot

A well-crafted plot must entice readers from the beginning. The conflict presented in the story must also be believable for readers. Each character will also have their own motives, but it's important that their motives are credible so that it adds to the story. Create enticing openings and hooks at the end of each chapter. Each scene should advance the plot or illuminates the character, or both.

It's important to avoid any coincidences as the story progresses because these are cop-outs for lazy writers. A common practice is to actively think of new ways to improve the story. Don't resort to plotless events that don't contribute anything significant to your plot.

Try to limit meandering introspection and use unexpected twists that engages your readers. Weaving subplots is another technique that experienced writers rely on. The older your audience, the more subplots you can create as they're likely to enjoy in-depth storytelling. Ensure that your story is factually correct too (if the story uses real-life elements).

Authors must play fair; there must be foreshadowing for readers to catch on. Avoid adding last-minute characters or solutions. Foreshadowing is a clue as to what might happen later. Another mistake inexperienced writers do might be using the most obvious solution, but this will only result in your readers being disappointed. Even if you are writing for young readers, it's good practice to let your story spark their imagination. Be consistent with time and space as well, as older readers might pick up on these smaller details.

Build confidence in the reader that the story will work out in the end, as young readers will appreciate an emotionally satisfying conclusion.

The challenging part for inexperienced writers is applying all of these rules. A perfect piece of writing has probably got all of these. Most will settle for less.

Structure

The structure of a story is its skeleton. The main bones include:
- An attention grabbing opening.
- Character, problem and setting introduced quickly.
- The boring but necessary bits in the middle.
- Foreshadowing or suggestions which are satisfactorily answered later.
- An interesting twist which ties up all the ideas.

Creating your story's characters

Characters are best created before attempting your opening. Devise a character dossier e.g., name, gender, age, appearance, family situation, job, likes, dislikes, hobbies, desires etc. Each of your characters should have some unusual/outstanding visual characteristic i.e., they don't always have to be human, but should have some human qualities. Main characters should be given a distinctive name that possibly suggests some unique characteristic that stands out.

Helpful hints on naming your characters

- Make the name appropriate to the personality e.g., Dash for a fast moving 10-year-old.
- Avoid using dated names e.g., Perceval.
- Avoid names that are difficult to pronounce or spell: e.g., Phoebe, Hugh, Morfydd.
- Don't give common names to villains.
- Avoid alliterative names in animal stories e.g., Peter Possum.
- Purchase a good name-the-baby book. Google, use phone directories, baby announcements or class rolls. But don't use a real first and family name together!
- Check the common names for certain cultures and write them in the acceptable order.

Creating a good opening

Good openers don't always begin at the beginning. Instead, they take the reader right into the action. Good openers are immediate, emotionally involving and make the reader want to read on.

Establish the major character, the problem or conflict facing that character and clue the reader as to the setting and time of the story. Avoid using a minor character at the start as this can confuse the reader. Limit the characters to one or two who will be easily distinguishable.

Contrast names, gender, personalities and distinguishing mannerisms. Cue the reader, but don't bore with minutiae. Treat the reader as an intelligent partner who enjoys strategically placed clues about characters.

Description needs to be subtly slipped into the action rather than introduced in a block at the beginning. A strategically placed verb or adjective can be far more effective than lines of predictable description.

Tense must be established. Although **present** is more immediate, technically, **past** is more manageable. Use the active rather than the passive voice. Dialogue is often a good way to throw the reader into the action.

Avoid long **paragraphs** especially on the first page. Wall-to-wall type is off-putting, particularly to a slow reader.

Sentence length is important, especially for a child reader. Vary length but ensure that the majority of sentences are short and grammatically simple. That is, one idea per sentence. Avoid writing a 'confetti' of ideas, random undeveloped thoughts.

Factual openings should not overdose on technical jargon. Define terms in the simplest way.

Be consistent in use of **viewpoint**. First person 'I' viewpoint may create an immediate emotional intimacy but later this viewpoint may become overwhelming. The more objective 3rd person 'he' or 'she' enables the writer to enter many characters' heads. The danger in rapid changes of character viewpoint leaves the reader confused and feeling emotionally disloyal.

Read the opening aloud for appropriate vocabulary, natural rhythm and intelligibility. If the book is for a certain age group, find a child of a similar age to read it aloud. Listen carefully, and rewrite where the child stumbles, mispronounces or yawns. Although it may be the opening, the introductory paragraph is probably the last piece polished. Make sure it remains consistent with the ending, especially if this has been redrafted several times.

Atmosphere and tone are particularly relevant. Details of plot and the emotional landscape of the book must be balanced out. The author must inspire confidence that every aspect of the fictitious world is under control. Use of coincidence, underdeveloped characters, emotional shifts without believable motives and an intruding authorial voice destroy confidence and atmosphere. If the author 'talks down' to children, the tone will act as a 'turn off' to any aged reader. A personal pact exists between author and reader irrespective of their individual ages. The author guarantees not to fake it.

In the same way as people mistakenly believe that writing a short story is easier than writing a novel, creating an introduction to a children's short story is not simple. Tight effective writing is necessary. A deceptively simple opening might have taken many, many rewrites. Analysing the technical components of a story is a challenge. However, to improve any story, the writer needs to be able to identify weaknesses or deficiencies. If unaware of certain techniques that best convey ideas, then it is difficult to identify absences.

Example of a good opening

NB. Characterisation through action and dialogue, viewpoint, setting and whether past or present tense is used.

> 'I've left Wilhelmina sitting in the NO STANDING zone,' said Auntie Viv. 'Since she's sitting not standing, I hope the van won't get booked.'
>
> 'Is Wilhemina one of your relatives?' asked the airport attendant politely.
>
> The twins laughed. 'Wilhelmina is a goat. She belongs to Auntie Viv's animal actors' business.'

Voice and viewpoint

Voice is the sound through which the reader hears and understands the action. This can be done in various ways:

1. First person voice and viewpoint (an 'I' viewpoint)

A strength is that the reader will be sympathetic to this character's situation. An 'I' viewpoint allows the reader to identify easily, but this emotional wallow can become overwhelming if the character is too self-centred, lacks self-deprecating humour or is predictable.

First person can be limiting because the reader only learns what that character is seeing and thinking. As a satirical device, a naive but likable 'super I' persona can be humorously used to criticise society.

If the 'I' is a major character in the story, it is easy to be in the centre of all of the action. But if 'I' is a minor character, it may be difficult for the writer to manipulate that character to learn all that he or she needs to know. The unfortunate limitation of using a minor character is that the character appears to be a gossip, an eavesdropper or a stickybeak.

The benefit of using a minor character's viewpoint is to obliquely dramatise the role of the real major character in the story. This is such a sophisticated device, that often the reader doesn't realise until the end, that the narrator was not the major character.

Since 'I' can be gender neutral if you're careful with other pronouns, it may be possible to sustain the suspense of revealing gender until the twist at the end.

2. Using a 'you' viewpoint

In practical terms, it is almost impossible to sustain a story written from the viewpoint of 'you'. The only benefit is that the generic 'you' can be singular or plural and this may provide a twist.

3. Third-person ('he' or 'she' or 'they') viewpoint

The third person viewpoint distances by simultaneously revealing how several characters think. A common mistake is to switch voices too quickly, particularly in short pieces. The reader finds this switch of allegiance frustrating. They'll tend to favour the character introduced first. If writers use very short sections, they can introduce more than one viewpoint a little more rapidly.

4. Omniscient (all-seeing) viewpoint

The omniscient viewpoint enables the writer to take the reader into the heads and motivations of all characters simultaneously.

5. Semi-omniscient viewpoint

A semi-omniscient viewpoint only pursues the ideas and thoughts of a few characters.

Language

Use the simplest and most appropriate word. Read aloud to check that the story flows. Trial it with an appropriately aged or skilled child. Find new ways of saying familiar things. Use verbs rather than adverbs or adjectives. The golden rule for choosing appropriate sentence length is, 'the younger the child, the shorter the sentence.'

Dialogue

Dialogue is more than breaking up the pattern on the page. Good dialogue:

- Shows instead of telling
- Interlinks with characterisation
- Fills in the background
- Creates vibrant paced reading.

Settings

Details of a setting must be accurate. In this case, using familiar settings are the easiest. So, it makes sense to use a workplace, sport venue or everyday location such as a shopping mall, the seaside or a fast-food outlet. Easy access means a writer can check on colour, shape, sound, smell, texture and taste.

An exotic setting may require expensive research to visit or photograph. Never use a well-known setting if it isn't familiar. If an important detail is left out, or something's wrong, a traveller will notice. Then the traveller-reader will disbelieve everything else.

Outlining chapters

Plan very carefully. Some writers draw up a flow chart or graph their characters' lives. Others write a minute-to-minute outline of each chapter. A few 'just go with the flow.' Here are some handy hints:

- If the plot is changed in midstream, remember to fix the opening.
- Don't think that 'meandering description' or 'fleshing-out' will maintain your reader's interest.
- Don't 'pad' to reach an acceptable word length. Shorter is usually better.
- Constantly recheck that a charcacter retains their unique characteristics, e.g., a character retains their 'black eyes and is left-handed'. Changing characteristics can be very confusing for readers.
- Pages of indirect speech can get very dull. Where possible, use direct speech. Juxtapose this with action and description.
- Perfect dialogue skills.
- Maintain the original conflict.
- Check for inconsistencies of time and space.
- Leave enough 'loose threads' to provide a satisfying ending.
- Weave unique subplot to create an enriching story.
- Check that subplots are relevant.
- Foreshadow the endings within important events in the story.

Creating enticing endings

Enticing endings gather all loose threads. (Hint: re-read to the second last chapter. On a pad, jot all clues, character traits and brief references which haven't been explained earlier. Go back and insert explanations, not always in the last chapter.) Good endings don't take too long to conclude and manages not to conclude the story too quickly.

A few questions can be left to the reader's imagination. However, the younger the reader, the more a satisfying conclusion is needed.

Happy endings, anyone? The fashion for unhappy endings in Young Adult (YA) literature is a matter of personal taste. The character can achieve the goal, miss out or emotionally adjust to not achieving it (maturity). But must be an emotionally satisfying ending for the reader.

Word limit

A picture story book is usually 32 pages. Occasionally it is 24 or 48 pages. This is due to multiples of historic 8-page bindings. The number of words varies from none to under 600. An initial draft may have more words, but once the illustrator has featured some of those ideas in the pictures, they can be deleted from the text, if the author agrees.

Picture book text for adolescents have more complex concepts, but the word numbers and structure are still simple. Also fashionable are comic graphic novels which vary in length but take considerable time for the illustrator to design dialogue and illustrate. Many more pages.

Illustrated stories are for newly independent readers. They are often known as chapter books, where each chapter should be approximately the same length. Book length varies from 4,000 to 10,000 words.

Hi-interest, simple-vocabulary books or 'second chance' readers are for remedial and English as a Second Language (ESL) students. Often these are fast paced with short sentences, simple vocabulary and interest level approximately 2 years higher than the reading level. This means that they are quite short; on average 3–4,000 words. The published book looks longer with wide margins, cartoon style illustrations and medium-sized print. Challenging to write but big readership via schools.

Junior novels, chapter books (age 8–11) and non-fiction can range between 8,000 to 30,000 words. Again, chapters should be roughly equal in length with intriguing titles. Non-fiction often include black and white line drawings and an accessible design is important.

Adolescent novels (age 11–13) and non-fiction will vary from approximately 8,000 to 35,000 words, though there is a trend to keep these shorter.

Young Adult (age 14+) novels vary in emotional complexity often resembling an adult novel in breadth and length. Length from 20,000 words upwards. Internationally the YA market goes up to early twenties readership.

Exercises

1. **Opener:** During a bushfire, a small boy loses his favourite toy. His older sibling is with him.

   After establishing the **setting** and **voice**, write the opening paragraph for:
   a. A story picture book
   b. A chapter book for young readers
   c. A Young Adult novel

2. **Plotting:** Draw up a story board for a 24-four-page illustrated picture book using an environmental theme.

3. **Characters:** Design a character dossier for Amadeus Brahms Scriabin, a musical rat. Give age, appearance, family, occupation, hobbies, likes, dislikes, friends, etc.

4. **Dialogue:** Rewrite the following situation in dialogue that will make it dramatic:

   Afraid of heights, Kit is on a school adventure camp where a teammate Chris needs rescuing as the narrow bridge across the gully breaks and there's only fast flowing water below. Chris is dangling on a safety rope. No-one else is around. No mobile reception.

5. **Ending:** Plot/re-write the ending, last page only, of an earlier MS of yours.
   a. As a picture story book
   b. As a chapter book for young readers
   c. As a Young Adult novel.

Checklist

Take any book and check for the following:

1. Does the plot entice from the first sentence?

_____

_____

2. Are the characters' motives credible?

3. Are the conflicts believable?

4. Any unbelievable coincidences?

5. Is the story plot-driven?

6. Any meandering introspection?

7. Any unexpected twists?

8. Is there an emotionally satisfying conclusion?

9. Any subplots, particularly in chapter books? What are they?

10. Any factual errors?

_____
_____

11. Any inconsistencies of time and space?

_____
_____

12. Is there any foreshadowing?

_____
_____

13. Does the end of each chapter have a 'hook'?

_____

After you've finished looking through other books, look through your own manuscript and check for the following:

1. Does your story have an attention-grabbing opening?

_____
_____

2. Are the character, problem and setting introduced quickly?

_____
_____

3. Are the necessary bits in the middle, boring or highly readable?

_____
_____

4. Are there any suggestions which are satisfactorily answered later?

_____
_____

5. Is there an interesting twist at the end which ties up all the ideas?

6. Does the dialogue show rather than tell?

7. In what ways does the dialogue add immediacy to the narrative?

8. To what extent are dialogue and characterisation interlinked?

9. Check the vocabulary. How appropriate is it for that age group?

10. To what extent does the prose have a rhythm when read aloud?

CHAPTER 11

Non-fiction

Why write and cater to the non-fiction market?

1. It is easier to sell than fiction

There's a consistent non-fiction market but facts must be accurate and often in prescribed formats of topics, lengths or language levels. It's easier to sell non-fiction manuscripts mainly because work is commissioned or at least discussed with the editor before the writer begins the project. Often the topic has to fit in with curriculum or a theme such as 'Scientific Discoveries' or 'Great Journeys'.

2. Non-fiction books are often contracted before writing starts

A non-fiction project may be written 'on spec', discussed or contracted with an agreed fee including an advance. A new writer may work 'on spec' which mean on speculation, hoping the subject of the manuscript will fit somewhere in some publisher's list. A 'discussion' with an editor may lead to 'slanting' the non-fiction subject to fit a theme, and thus increase the likelihood of it being selected and including in the series publications.

3. Less time and energy consuming than fiction

The most time and energy effective way of working is on commissioned works. Since non-fiction is typically commissioned, it is generally less time and energy consuming. An agreement is reached on the subject, length, deadline, audience and fee, before the work is done. This may occur even when the writer initiated the subject because of a personal interest in researching it or specialised knowledge.

4. It's less challenging than writing fiction books

From some authors' viewpoints, the challenge of collecting and 'ordering' information rather than 'imagining' fictitious scenarios, is preferable. Others get double value out of their research and re-use (recycle) it as fictional background in later stories.

Examples of non-fiction writing

The following is an excerpt taken from an interview with Audrey, who owned a business which released doves for special occasions. Using the Q and A technique is a way of concentrating information.

Working With Doves

Q. How do you make sure the doves fly home?

Audrey: We train them. At least twice a week. On training runs they learn to fly home from all directions. For the Australia Day spire launch, we trained them for two weeks by working out a direct line from the spire to home. Then we'd release them at different points along that route. Birds come home to be paid, that's when they're fed. Pigeons have an internal navigation system. They use sun or stars to navigate but they're backed up by an awareness of magnetic lines or force. Like a GPS. They fly back to their pigeon cote. They don't need a street directory.'

Q. Do doves ever drop on the bride?

Audrey: No. We 'dry them out' by not feeding or watering them immediately before a wedding. Then they fly home afterwards for drink and food.

Q. If doves are released at a wedding inside a building, where do they fly to?

Audrey: Our doves are trained to fly back to the trainer who is standing there.

Q. How do you get 100 birds ready for big occasions?

Audrey: I used to buy white doves at the bird auctions, but now I breed our own. The quality is better. We wash them and make them look beautiful before their flights.

Q. Do any get lost flying home?

Audrey: Occasionally we'd lose one or two. One bird took two days to struggle home when he had been attacked by a big bird.

Q. At a wedding, can children hold your doves?

Audrey: Yes. Children always want to take our doves home. They love holding them. At one wedding, two birds sat on the head of a guest. She loved it.

Q. Why do you release a dove at a funeral?

Audrey: Releasing a dove at the graveside, gracefully symbolises the release of that person's spirit, whatever their religious beliefs.

Q. What do you do with the dove at a funeral?

Audrey: Outstretching my hands, I hold the dove with a trailing, white ribbon as I stand at the head of the grave. When the celebrant calls for the release of the spirit, I open my hands and let the dove fly upwards. The white ribbon flutters back to earth. A dove is a natural symbol of comfort.

Q. What if the best thing about having 'Doves of Peace'?

Audrey: Seeing people's happy faces when they hold or look at the birds.

Censorship: One magazine rejected this article because it was thought that funerals should not be mentioned in a children's magazine.

Arranging a table of contents

A table of contents is usually confined to non-fiction:

- Common questions about the subject may be used as chapter headings. Include sub-headings to indicate the content and help you organise your material initially.
- An adult might feel embarrassment about asking questions considered personal, impertinent or inappropriate. However, most 10-year-olds are genuinely interested in how things work. During a Grade 6 excursion to a funeral parlour, one boy genuinely asked, 'If a hearse is used for her, what is used for him?'

- Often there will be a catchy title and then an informative subtitle on the cover.
- Start with the most interesting information, finish with the second most interesting, and 'bury' the boring bit in the middle.
- Think about how it might be structured. Chronologically? Thematically? FAQs? As a quest to find the answer?
- Consider the possible layout. Print size? Illustrations? Photographs? Charts? Diagrams? Cartoons?
- If there is access to expertise in scientific, photographic or illustrative areas, indicate this on the proposal.

Considerations for writing non-fiction

1. Don't assume that your 'highly talented' 17-year-old daughter's artwork fits the bill. Including substandard or inaccurately designed artwork may handicap your concept.

2. Don't just scan/copy technical diagrams from other published works. You may be breaking copyright rules. You will need permission (with or without a fee) to use existing professional photographs.

Examples of creating a table of contents

Here is the Table of Contents of a non-fiction book on a scientific subject aimed at under 12s. Many of the chapter headings are based around questions.

Pyrotechnics: How Fireworks Got Off the Ground

Table of Contents

- Collage of Comments
- Who Does What?
- Sky Shows
- Recipe for a Sky Show
- Computer-Aged Fireworks: Interview with Pyro-Technician
- In the Past
- What are Pyro-Technics?
- Types of Fireworks
- How to Photograph Fireworks
- Smoke on the Water. Fire in the Sky

- Why Does It Explode?
- How are Fireworks Coloured?
- How Does a Rocket Work?
- Black Powder
- People and Fireworks
- How is Smoke Made in a Theatre?
- Safety

It would be necessary to indicate the photographs and their possible sources, and whether permissions and fees are necessary.

Exercises

1. Imagine a scenario where you are a 10-year-old wanting to learn about prosthetics.
   a. List down the 10 most common questions you'd be likely to ask a prosthetics maker (designer and maker of false limbs)
   b. Now turn these questions into prospective chapter headings.
   c. Think of a title and subtitle for the factual book covering a day in the life of a prosthetist (prosthetics maker).
2. Choose a marine topic for a highly illustrated or photographic book of the Great Barrier Reef.
   a. List the Table of Contents and include a suggested art brief that is a one-page letter of suggestions for the photographer or illustrator to follow.
   b. Indicate prospective age group of readership and number of pages.

NB. Remember the importance of inserting an index and a Bibliography.

Checklist

1. Is your piece of non-fiction checked with an expert and a non-expert (naive) reader? Or checked with a sensitivity reader?

   _____
   _____
   _____

2. Is the piece aimed at an educational market? If so, is the language, tone and length appropriate for a particular age group?

   _____
   _____
   _____

3. Is the table of contents detailed and intriguing?

_____

_____

_____

4. Is a bibliography or links necessary?

_____

_____

_____

5. How up to date is the piece? Are the current year's figures in there?

_____

_____

_____

6. Has an illustrator's brief been prepared suggesting appropriate diagrams, photos and illustrations?

_____

_____

_____

7. Do you have a contract and an advance?

_____

_____

_____

CHAPTER 12

A good title sells

Features of a good title

Effective titles need to be memorable, unexpected, informative, engaging and witty. That's a lot to expect from a word or phrase. There will probably be many working titles but occasionally, a title will fit immediately. Often, help will be given from the marketing department: whether asked for or not. Because so many books are published, marketing needs your title to 'stand out' from competitors. So the need to 'draw attention' may differ from the author's desire to indicate the book's content or tone.

The marketing department of the biggest publishers will always demand a title with all these features:

- Provocative title that can attract media attention
- Signals what is inside the book and be able to imply success or fun
- Easily distinguishable to stand out from competitors
- Having an interesting cover design with a unique title
- Enable the reps to sell on sight
- Appropriate key words for search engine optimisation (SEO)
- Uses apt language for target readership
- Title that's easily pronounced
- Entices readers into thinking that information is unique to the book and isn't available anywhere else.

Ambiguous, witty, one-word titles are in demand. But they're very hard to create. What are some other options?

- Using common phrases e.g., Working Things Out
- Altering by changing to a negative. e.g., Not Working Things Out
- A subtitle linking three objects where the third one is unexpected e.g., Words, Speakers and Bores
- Something unexpected like using a number, but whether it should be in figures or words is a disadvantage e.g., 6788.

One of the main challenges in naming a book is to ensure that all ambiguities are relevant e.g., people may get confused as to whether this is a book about writing FOR children or writing BY children. This needs to be made clear. In our case this book is for adults. So stressing the business side, becomes very relevant.

Naming books is harder than naming babies. In the same way that playground nicknames overtake parent-chosen names, author suggestions are increasingly overtaken by 'marketing' departments of publishing houses. Authors often find themselves in a delicate dance with their publishers, as the marketing department's expertise in branding and audience appeal becomes a driving force in title selection.

Striking a balance between artistic integrity and commercial viability remains a challenge, reminding authors that naming books is indeed a unique art form in itself.

Exercises

For the following imaginary manuscript, find appropriate and catchy titles:

1. **Non-fiction**
   a. A children's guide to planting a vegetable garden.
   b. A guide to carrying out small scientific experiments at home.
   c. A guide showing how to design a home office in a remote area.
2. **Fiction**
   a. A chapter mystery for young readers featuring guide dog training and a failed therapy dog called Min who was scared of traffic.
   b. Rom and Julie fall in love but are thwarted by rival gangs.
   c. A sci-fi horror featuring alien insects.

Checklist

Will the title of your book:

1. Be provocative?

   _____
   _____

2. Attract media attention?

   _____
   _____

3. Signal what's inside?

   _____
   _____

4. Imply sex, success, money or fun? (Whichever qualities are relevant to the age group.)

5. Be easily distinguishable?

6. Lend itself to an interesting cover design?

7. Enable the publishing representative to sell it on sight?

8. Use apt language for that readership?

9. Be easily pronounced?

10. Be memorable?

CHAPTER 13

Reworking and writing drafts

Clearing mental space

No one likes having to do more drafts. If only a piece of writing could be perfect at the first go. Some writers argue that they mentally edit. First off, they can write the perfect and final version. Others think on paper, or on screen, writing six or eight versions before the final draft is personally acceptable. Then the editor may demand other changes.

Redrafting

1. Plan mental space by working on several projects simultaneously. Writers often have a first draft of one piece of work, at the same time tackling the second or third draft of another MS. Consider leaving the MS for long enough to review with the eyes of a new reader.
2. Find an honest reader/critic whose constructive suggestions you'd consider.
3. Workshop the MS so that it can be read aloud by someone else. Follow the reading on another copy. Remove repetitious sounds, e.g., too many S sounds, overused favourite words, clichés, purple prose and overwriting – especially description. Good prose is like good music. It must have rhythm, style and pace.

4. How many drafts are acceptable? The answer is, how much time can you afford to spend. Ask these questions:

   Can you afford not to spend time on it?

   What are its chances of being published in a rough version? Unless the writer is well known, in this present economic market, the answer is 'not many'.

5. How much better will its chances be if the MS is reworked? This is the freelancer's gamble. Balancing these variables:

   Time spent v Income v Publication v Reputation.

6. Depending on the situation, it may be feasible to send out a MS that is 90% ready to a highly likely market, rather than spend another week refining it. However, if the work is aimed at a 'literary' market, the final polishing will be vital.

Helpful hints

- Consistency of voice may be a particular problem to solve when redrafting. Using a juvenile 1st person voice may take a number of drafts to ensure consistency.
- Complexity of plot. In a genre novel like a mystery, threads, clues and 'red herrings' need to be checked when redrafting.
- Label files so they can be distinguished between different drafts. It's embarrassing to email a previous version. Retain old drafts on file – carefully labelled and dated. (Bonus: If it should happen to be a best-seller, this will be proof that 'it's all the writer's own work.' Also useful for a literary biographer.)
- What tends to happen with several versions of one work is that the first draft is short but has spontaneity. The second draft will flesh out minor details but tends to be over long. The third may be the final, polished version, or may have lost the spontaneity.

Exercises

1. Take anything recently written and read it aloud.
   a. Ask someone else to *silently* read it. Note if they read it right through or become distracted.
   b. Ask for the draft to be read *aloud*. Note on another copy where the reader falters.
   c. What is your story about? Summarise the MS into a short, short paragraph. Is the direction of the story/piece always clear? If not, rethink.
   d. Check grammar, spelling and sentence length.
   e. Are there long chunks of descriptive prose that might work better as direct speech?
   f. Put the MS aside for a while, then use an editor's pencil or tracking. Tracking enables you to have a feeling of accomplishment that you have improved the coloured tracking parts. Be stringent. Often the favourite description is entirely unnecessary.

Checklist

1. How many separate MS are you presently working on?

2. Do you have an 'honest' critic? Can you befriend one?

3. How well can you take criticism? Remember, no one's criticising you, just the MS.

4. Have you had someone else read the work aloud?

5. Is the voice consistent? Is it easy to read? E.g., Are there too many sibilants?

6. Check your grammar, spelling and punctuation.

7. Is the plot easy to follow and logical? Have you tied up all your loose ends?

8. Do you still have access to carefully labelled previous drafts?

9. Has your final draft retained that spontaneity?

10. Give it one final read aloud. Then send it!

CHAPTER 14

Marketing

Market research

'Marketing' is the fancy name for 'selling'. Title, cover, blurb, bio-notes, reviews and general appearance all contribute to book sales. Digital books, like eBooks rely even more heavily on only title and cover due to limited listings online.

Two types of marketing

1. The selling of a particular book to a particular audience
   e.g., a picture book to a picture book audience, or to young audience and associated parents, teachers and librarians.
2. Simultaneously, the author is being judged as an author-business person by publishers and media. An author must be able to supply biographical notes and photographs, punctuality and presentation – an author is allowed to be quirky in appearance, but never to be late for live air interviews. Publishers require an author to be articulate, obliging about autographing sessions, quick to reply to children's letters and discreet. In other words, professional.

Professional competence

No artist or musician can succeed without professional training. But because everybody writes and everybody has been a child, writing for children is seen as highly accessible to amateurs.

Due to their workplace isolation, authors tend to be notorious gossipers whenever they meet others in the industry. In the small literary world, indiscretion can be bad for business. So whatever happens, avoid complaining about the following:

- Inefficient publishers or publishers who don't reprint quickly enough
- Missing out to your book being shortlisted
- Envious of award-winning authors
- Booksellers not stocking your titles
- Your books not being more prominent in bookshops
- Lack of reviews and the 'incompetence of reviewers'
- Royalties, advances, prize money, grants – or the lack of all of these
- How much other authors make or giving a personal opinion of how they did it
- Don't pass on literary gossip told in confidence
- Even if your book is financially successful and 'in demand', don't boast under the guise of 'I've got too much to do'
- Don't have a short-term affair with your publisher, publicist or literary colleagues.

Maintaining good practices

After learning to avoid all the pitfalls, it's good practice to do the following:

- Distinguish between a subjective reaction to an MS being rejected, or not being invited to a literary market or function and the objective reality of a small market and too many contenders.
- Be generous in genuine praise of other writers.
- Encourage up and coming writers.
- Have prepared responses for ignorant comments like:
    - 'When are you going to write a real book?'
    - 'Do you get paid for writing little books like that?'
    - 'Bet you knocked that out in five minutes.'
    - 'I'm sure your grandchildren enjoy your stories.'
- For these needs strategic replies, such as:
    - 'I write for adults and children. However, writing for children is technically more difficult.'

- 'Australian children's authors consistently earn more export dollars than most adult authors and are more influential in spreading Australian culture.'
- 'It's a mistake to assume the IQ of the writer is tied to the age of the reader.'
- 'I regard myself as a professional. And I make a living from my writing skills.'

Marketing strategies

When it comes to marketing strategies, offer something extra or different.

1. For educational titles, offer thematic activities and/or teacher discussion notes and links to the curricula.
2. Suggest innovative and child-centred launches which are likely to attract publicity. Launch your book online, although an online launch often limits opportunities for sales of hard copies or adds postage costs.
3. Suggest links with other mediums e.g., books can link into radio/TV/stage performance/multimedia-digital options.
4. Provide the publicist with a background article on research which can be used as data for a feature article.
5. Have something visual to show for television interviews e.g., a puppet or intriguing (small) finding from your research.
6. When interviewed, always mention title and publisher.
7. Link with a topical celebration or anniversary e.g., the designated United Nations Year. Or use multi-cultural custom such as 'name days'.
8. Publicise the innovative way a MS was written. Possibly the use of co-writers; where the writing took place; the medium used.
9. If it's a picture book or uses illustrations, display the artwork in a gallery, library or foyer of a relevant building.
10. Have your cover and research visuals to show in the latest format for big talks.

The ongoing marketing of an 'author image' as a professional is very important. In a large organisation this is a corporate image. Since a creative business relies on the way others perceive an individual's skills, talent and output, their perception depends on how professional the writer seems.

Is the author seen as a creative dabbler in the arts? Or as a competent practitioner in the business of ideas? Never use the excuse of 'being creative' to cover your inefficiencies. However, it is difficult for a person who draws on internal resources to maintain a constant sense of professionalism. During lean times – such as when there are many rejections, or a big project has to be sustained without outside praise or reinforcement – the author will need some form of self-evaluation.

Some authors keep weekly lists of 'achievements' and 'flops'. Don't expect perfection, just progress.

An even more important aspect of marketing is what is said about a book by the writer and by other people. Even before the book appears, interest needs to be generated. What makes this book worth space on air or online? In newspaper review columns? On TV chat shows? The reality is that for children's books, unless the subject matter is controversial or the author is well known, the book is probably not covered in the general media, but maybe mentioned in online blogs and newsletter links. If the author is accessible and well prepared, this will help increase the book's chances of coverage.

A new writer will need background information available. Often, you will be asked for a bio or a hi-res photo or a bibliography. Have them downloadable under Media Resources on your author website. Keep an electronic clippings file of reviews or PR about published books – it may be a necessary reference/source for future quotes to go on blurbs.

Creating a corporate image

Creating a corporate image is essential for any aspiring writer. To create one, you need to prepare a formal Curriculum Vitae (CV). This should feature:

- Personal details e.g., name, address, phone number, author website, email address
- List of published work
- A brief work history including writing and non-writing occupations

- Interests and expertise including qualifications
- Relevant study in this area.

A crisp biographical note written in the third person as 'he' or she' or gender diverse 'they' not as 'I'. You may have different types of bios for different readerships e.g., one written for an Under 12 reader and another for an adult market. Children are more interested in the gossipy details like whether the writer keeps pets, favourite food, favourite colour or word, 'your children' and 'do they read your stories?' or 'are your own children 'in' any of the books?'

When maintaining a corporate image, you will need a professional, digital photo in various resolutions. Often 'studio corporate formal' photos are not seen as appropriate for an author who needs to appeal to a young readership. Maybe an informal, outside shot with a pet, but make the contrast clear. Also include the name of the photographer for a professional credit. If the photo was taken by a newspaper or magazine photographer, permission for publicity use, credits and a fee may need to be arranged.

If the author has more than one publisher, have different photos to use for publicity purposes, so keep track of where certain photos have been used. And which book you are holding. Update every two years, so real life bears some resemblance to the age of the photo and your face.

A collage kit of book covers, reviews and profiles or features which relates to each book title or project may save time when the author become a 'project' for a student or publishers need reviewers' 'quotes' to use on blurbs. Always source your material with date and publication.

Manuscript (MS) presentation

Your manuscript must always include a synopsis. The manuscript should also provide the following:

- It describes the kind of book this is: theme/style/potential reader.
- Includes the story title and outstanding characteristic.
- The main character's major problem, setting, time and place.
- Should consist of only one page, double-spaced, of about 250 words.

- Presents the conflict or summary of the plot.
- A resolution to the presented conflict.
- Language and style aimed at an adult audience.

A MS should cover the following technical aspects:

- Good quality A4 paper but nowadays is usually submitted electronically.
- Has double spacing, single sided, paged numbers and wide margins. Do not justify the right-hand margin.
- Do not use italics. Underline in the conventional way when you intend the printed page to show italics.
- Indent paragraphs as usual.
- Use single quotation marks.
- No spelling errors. Make sure that spelling, hyphenation, capitalisation etc. are consistent. Beware of relying on computer spell checks.
- Use minimum capitals for chapter headings.
- Story title in *every* page.
- Your name on every page.
- Send a single page cover letter with your manuscript.
- Manuscript must be contained. It is vital that your manuscript be impeccably presented – a clean, professionally presented manuscript has the edge over sloppy work.
- Keep a hard and electronic copy of your story.
- Most publishers will acknowledge receipt of your manuscript within days. Allow several months for notification of a decision about your manuscript.
- Digital publication is faster and eBooks can be published within a few months.

Exercises

Be prepared to answer any questions sent by children's magazine son behalf of fans, as they will want to get to have a better picture of who you are as a person. Some typical questions they might send are:

1. What is your full name?
2. Where were you born?
3. What is your favourite colour?
4. What is your favourite food?
5. What is your favourite book that you wrote?
6. What's your favourite book that someone else wrote?
7. What are your hobbies?
8. Have you got any children?
9. Do they ever read your books?
10. Have they ever said anything bad about what you've written?
11. Where do you live?
12. What football team do you follow?
13. Can I have your autograph?
14. What book are you working on now?
15. How do you choose the names of your characters?
16. How much money do you make?
17. Where do you get your ideas?
18. How did you feel when your first book was published?
19. How does your family feel about you being a writer?
20. Do people recognise you in the supermarket?

Checklist

For your new MS:

1. Are you offering something different or extra, such as a thematic activity linked to the curricula?

_____

2. Have you prepared some background articles?

_____

_____

3. Do you have something visual to present at launches and talks?

_____

_____

4. How well do you respond to an interviewer? Practise with a friend.

_____

_____

5. Have you found some innovative way to discuss how your story was written?

_____

_____

6. Do you have any artwork e.g., a blown up cover or internal illustrations, to allow your audience to focus on while you speak? Places like Officeworks make retractable banners in various sizes.

_____

_____

7. Have you written your bio notes?

_____

_____

8. In what ways have you got some discussion going about your book before it appears?

_____

_____

9. If you are asked to read a selection from your book, how well can you do this? Keep it SHORT! Practise reading aloud. Reading aloud is as much a craft as performing a piece of music.

_____

_____

CHAPTER 15

Coping with rejection

Receiving rejection from publishers

Rejections can be sent in many ways:

- The rejecting editor just ticks a box
- The rejecting editor sends a form letter and fills your name and MS at the top
- The rejecting editor returns your MS and it looks unread
- No response at all
- Feedback. If so, act on it and rewrite.

All writers receive rejection slips. Some talk more freely about them than others. On reflection, a writer may admit to sending out a manuscript when it really needed more work.

Strategies for coping

This isn't an exhaustive list of all the ways you can cope but take it as a general guide and try out what works for you to learn from the rejection and use it to improve your next project.

1. Ask: Was it the wrong time, the wrong place, the wrong format?
2. Reread, rewrite and submit to another publisher.

3. Add something to the MS. For an educational publisher itemise links to the curricula. In other words suggest specific ways teachers can use it.
4. Give it to an informed critic and act on the suggestions.
5. Repackage the MS to look more attractive.
6. Change the title. Add a subtitle.
7. Keep redrafting until the MS is sold.
8. Cannibalise the MS and use it in another project.
9. Accept that this MS isn't saleable at this time and place.
10. If the concept isn't sold after exhausting the possible commercial market, allow it to be used in a non-paying publication. But retain the copyright and add it the CV.
11. Write it off to experience and start something new.
12. Try digital formats.

Self-publishing

More and more people are self-publishing books these days. Technological advancements have made it easier. However few self-published books do very well but normally are a great option for authors who want complete control of their work. Self-publishing may be an option if you:

- Are energetic
- Have cash resources
- Know a niche market
- Have distribution channels
- Have plenty of time
- Have desktop publishing access and skills
- Have project management skills
- Have space to store books
- Are firmly convinced that the writing is good enough
- Self-promote well.

Join a writing group

Joining a writing group can help broaden what you know and gives you an opportunity to connect with like-minded individuals. You benefit not only from receiving input from other professionals, but you can also provide input to help others.

1. Members need to be equal in output, but their skills can be different. They need to be equivalent in skill, sophistication, energy, experience and income level.
2. A loose organisation works better than one with too many rules, obligations, and regulations.
3. Regular but flexible meeting dates preferably planned a year ahead.
4. Rotate responsibilities for organising. Keep the time and location the same.
5. Limit the gossip to the first ten minutes. Have a place with good acoustics and plenty of space to move around.
6. A 'meal meeting' saves time, but don't make the catering competitive.
7. Comment on the MS, not the writer. Manuscript rejection by a publisher, face to face work-shopping criticism and adverse reviews or certain moral stances culminating in censorship, are not quite the same. But the effect on the author/creator can be equally devastating.
8. It is wise to remind the group members that the work, NOT the person, is being critiqued.
9. When reading another member's work, offer productive criticism. Try not to be destructive.
10. Another form of rejection is moral criticism of the content. This maybe entirely subjective on the part of the critic. The rejection may take the form of public criticism, agitating to have certain books withdrawn from libraries, or overly critical reviews.

There are different types of rejection. Anonymous rejection by an unknown publisher via a letter or form is less personal than being part of a critique group where the people are familiar and commenting personally about that piece of work. However, being part of a writing group generally improves the quality of writing, provides a forum and softens the rejection by providing constructive alternatives.

Ethical dilemmas

Being misinterpreted is a common problem for a writer. It may mean that the writing or logic was sloppy, or that societal attitudes have changed, or the reader has fixed views. As a result, the reader gets upset about something inferred from the author's work. Ironically, children's authors are expected to be 'morally pure' and are therefore more likely to be criticised for their choice of language, subject, their moral stance or lack of it. Often an adult is criticising on behalf of a hypothetical 'perfect and innocent' child who may not even have read that book, yet.

Sometimes the writer has not intended to offend the reader, yet the reader has taken what is written as a personal affront. There's not much anyone can do about that. Creating anything for public view: paintings, photos, sculpture, leaves the work open to comment. It has been suggested that one only offends when something is strongly felt. Offending for offense's sake, particularly in children's literature, is usually a problem of 'bad taste' (in terms of language, tone or subject matter that's usually subjective).

Censorship, both overt and insidious, occurs in the world of children's writing. Often a small group with strong views will insist that a book be withdrawn from a library. Or that the author is not entitled to write about a particular culture or sexual orientation without personal experience. Often 'causes' are espoused where only the subject matter is looked at, not the quality of the writing. Because it is a book about X, it is seen as 'acceptable or not acceptable', rather than how well it has been written or researched. Vocal minorities often swamp apathetic majorities and some publishers 'play safe' by rejecting any potentially controversial subjects or 'make a cause' out of their stance.

'Hot' topics include non-Indigenous writers drawing on researched Indigenous stories, creationists insisting that witches and Halloween lead to the 'occult', 'trans, gay and lesbian perspective', 'drug-violence', 'suicide' and 'true crime' stories. Some publishers overreact and anticipating criticism include a 'token' title on their list.

Indirectly the 'censorship' affects authors who realise that certain subject matter is less likely to be published. If they are experienced, high-profile authors they may punt on their name and writing quality carrying an unpopular subject because they genuinely feel the story should be written to give a balanced perspective for young readers. Unless the controversial subject is a 'first-person' account by a new writer and made into a 'publicity cause' by the publisher, beginners are unlikely to break in with a subject attracting censor. Consequently, the informal censoring limits certain types of material being available to young readers.

Drawing too closely from life and using it as a form of revenge is not to be recommended. The published word may seem a marvellous form of revenge and is sometimes used as part of a murder plot by novelists. However, in real life, the repercussions can be libellous, nasty and the writer might finally wish to 'take it all back.'

Not checking facts in highly technical material, is unforgivable. Non-fiction purports to be accurate. Sadly, these facts are often obsolete before the book/article even goes to press. However, every writer must make the greatest effort to check that what is written is as accurate and up to date as possible.

Exercises

1. The best exercise is to place a rejected MS in a drawer for a minimum of 6 months. Otherwise:
    a. Read other published pieces for the same age on a similar topic.
    b. Ask a friendly writer's group to workshop the piece as if it doesn't belong to you, the writer.
    c. Listen very carefully. Remember that they are criticising your piece, not the writer.
    d. Write something different before redrafting a rejected piece. Come to it with a fresh perspective.
    e. Is it possible to add something to the piece conceptionally? Maybe a page on how it connects with the curriculum.

Checklist

1. Have you sent your MS to the wrong publisher? Or written it in the wrong format?

   _____

   _____

2. Have you reread your MS, rewritten and submitted to the next publisher on your list?

   _____

   _____

3. Have you added something extra to the MS? Can you suggest specific ways in which educators can use it?

   _____

   _____

4. Have you given it to an informed critic and acted on the suggestions?

5. Did you repackage the MS to look more attractive?

6. Can you improve the title?

7. Will you keep on redrafting until the MS is sold?

8. If all else fails, can you cannibalise your MS and use it in another project?

9. Can you learn to accept that this MS isn't saleable at this time and place?

10. Can you write it off to experience and start something new?

CHAPTER 16

Collaborating and ghosting

Creating a successful collaboration

Writers tend to ask, 'why bother to collaborate with another writer?' Collaborating can be useful for various things:

1. Extending skills: by working together, it's possible to learn from someone with equal but different skills e.g., highly computer literate writing partner teaches the 'creative' one how to improve manuscript layout and use email attachments, Dropbox for hi-res files etc, saving travelling time. Or one writer might have 'technical' knowledge which saves having to research. The other can write in an accessible way for this audience.
2. Offers variety: collaboration counters the isolation of working alone and allows some 'fun' in the workstyle.
3. To overcome procrastination: obligation to have contribution ready for the next meeting.
4. The opportunity to work with a professional from another field can help to learning a new perspective. Often writers think in abstract or in words, actors may think in movement, sound, time or shape.
5. Strategic use of time, especially for tight deadlines. Collaborative works allows you to specialise in what you do best, while having another specialist to cover your weak areas.

6. To substitute or represent each other in business meetings or in marketing.
7. To find out how others work on a day-to-day basis. To compare 'how much is enough?'.
8. Marketing becomes easier because each collaborator has a set of different networks.

Literary collaborations are similar to marriages. Some work well. Others end in acrimony or in the divorce courts. Unfortunately, many collaborations don't work. But with some planning, the split could have been avoided. Most common problem areas are:

- Either when the project looks like being highly successful and one attempts to claim all the credit.
- Or if the project takes longer or is more difficult than at first envisaged.

Aspects of unsuccessful collaborations

Unsuccessful collaboration inevitably occurs to every writer. However, there are some points to look out for to avoid future unsuccessful collaborations:

- Initial agreement (or brief) was misinterpreted by at least one collaborator.
- Workstyles or pace are different. One is always late or disorganised.
- No letter of agreement was signed initially. Vital to decide who is going to own what of the percentages. Often, it's genuinely difficult to remember who actually thought of which idea. It's best to split the proceeds 50/50 regardless.
- Ethical dilemmas: inappropriate behaviour, lying, committing resources on behalf of the project without agreement. Running up bills for expensive printing, recording or travel.
- Because of fears of criticism, one partner is unable to finish and wants to 'let the project go'. While the work is still 'in progress', public scrutiny can be delayed.
- Too many collaborators. Either they don't agree or can't arrange for everybody to meet at one time.

- Quality varies. Some work is not as good as the other, and reputations are at stake.
- Incompatible styles of writing or working.
- Disorganisation. No clear aims, deadlines or agreed outcomes.
- Too much talk about what is 'going to happen' and not enough actual work.
- Jealousy about writing relationship or intrusions by partners or family.
- Some new amateurs start with initial enthusiasm which the other more experienced partner misinterprets as ability to get the project done.
- The amateur misses deadlines or 'plays the victim' of having a more demanding home life etc., and the more experienced collaborator does all the work rather than damage own reputation.

Once you've noted these guidelines down, always remember not to collaborate with another creator unless:

- Co-operating temperaments exist
- One collaborator can attend to details
- A regular time and place to work has been established
- Both writers recognise each other's strength and weaknesses
- Consideration of geographical limitations. Will too much time be wasted in travelling? Is email, Skype, Zoom or other digital exchanges possible?
- A co-signed letter of agreement or memorandum of understanding.

Collaborating online

Collaborating online offers a dynamic and efficient way to work together, whether it's through co-writing with digital attachments or leveraging the latest digital devices. One significant benefit is the time-saving aspect, as it eliminates the need for physical meetings and allows contributors to work on a project simultaneously, regardless of their geographic location. Moreover, online collaboration enables international partnerships, which not only enriches the diversity of ideas but also broadens the pool of expertise, making it easier to tackle complex projects that require specialised knowledge from different regions.

Pointers for productive partnerships

Choosing the 'right' partner isn't an easy task, but there are various ways to make an existing collaboration productive. Consider the following list as a guide:

- Choose writing partners as carefully as a romantic relationship.
- Choose a partner whose strengths complement, not mirror e.g., if one is a left-brain logical person with good attention to detail, the other may be a right-brain, intuitive thinker, perhaps a bit scatty about details but who sees the big picture and has original ideas.
- Look at the quality of the person's earlier work. Any credits which prove they finish to a quality standard? Have they collaborated before? Was it successful? By whose evaluation? Did they get it finished and keep to deadlines?
- Be specific about the scope, deadline, and quality of the project. Sign an agreement about rights.

Ghost writers

A ghost writer offers writing skills and manages the book project usually for an upfront fee and no public acknowledgment nor ongoing royalties. Often journalists are asked to ghostwrite for famous figures in their area of expertise e.g., a sports' journalist might be invited to ghostwrite an autobiography of a famous athlete. A pop singer who lacks time or words may need a ghost writer. Politicians' memoirs are often ghostwritten. Pro-ghosts are in demand and can negotiate to have a credit on the cover. It can be labelled as: *THE STORY OF X*, as told to …

A children's author who moonlights as a ghost writer, might be commissioned to write for a Young Adult audience. One variation of ghosting is when the major series-editor's name appears on a series of books. However, some will have been written by a 'pro-ghost'. Occasionally the major writer-editor will 'storyboard' the plot and the pro-ghost will flesh out the novel.

Professional writing organisations have suggested costings and contracts for ghosting. Often these projects take longer than expected because the 'famous subject' is not available due to travel work commitments or objections to the style.

Exercise

1. Initiate a 'ghost' writing project.
2. Offer to collaborate on a project, with an expert.
3. Research the 'going rate' for ghosting from a professional writing organisation. Find out how many is required to finish the project on deadline.

Checklist

1. Do you have a project which could use a collaborator?
   _____
   _____
   _____

2. What skills do you need in this partner?
   _____
   _____
   _____

3. What skills do you have to offer?
   _____
   _____
   _____

4. What is your deadline?
   _____
   _____
   _____

5. How long is the project? In research? In words? In time?

_____

_____

_____

6. Have you drafted a letter of agreement? Will the agreement be 50/50? If not, what is the ratio and why?

_____

_____

_____

7. Do you have publisher interest offering a contract? If not, which of you will 'pitch' the project, and where?

_____

_____

_____

CHAPTER 17

Reviews, critics and the media

Dealing with reviews, listings and critics

Once work becomes public, it will attract attention. Unfortunately, sometimes the reactions are neutral or unfavourable. A writer's etiquette is to not reply personally in public to a reviewer. The reality is that the children's literary world is very small. Judges and reviewers are supposed to be professionally neutral. So, what can one do about unjust criticism based on incorrect facts?

1. Remain silent and fume.
2. Ask a colleague to write a reply.
3. Tackle on grounds of facts not opinion. A letter to the editor could be an appropriate way of dealing with this.

One of the problems with children's books, is the limited exposure they receive in print via newspapers, magazines, online or on air. Not only are they mentioned infrequently, but the reviews are often so short, they are almost listings.

Increasingly, unpaid bloggers review print and eBooks online. Often blog-tours are mutually congratulatory listings on each other's sites. This provides faster publicity for a title than print reviewing. Sometimes these commentators have little knowledge of contemporary work for children and can't put the book in context of the writer's previous work or similar books.

What 'unsophisticated' reviewers often do – that is, someone not exposed to contemporary work – is relate their current reading to what they read as a child or what they wanted the author to write. Or they have a particular moral issue about which they feel strongly, like motherhood qualifying them to talk on all issues relating to all children. 'Mummy Bloggers' can be very influential. 'Culturally appropriate' bloggers can be influential too, where they promote any title which relates to their culture, regardless of the quality of writing or illustration.

Important to distinguish between political propaganda and objectively supporting the promotion of quality books which portray minority cultures.

A good book reviewer would share these characteristics:

- Reads the whole book before writing down their review.
- Have previously read other books targeted for that age group.
- Doesn't just paraphrase the blurb or the media handout.
- Encourages parents/librarians to be a little more adventurous in their buying.
- Points out the strength and weaknesses of characterisation, plot, ideas, title, etc.
- Doesn't just tell what the plot is.
- Relates to authors' previous work.
- Doesn't review only the 'good ones'.
- Doesn't judge the ethnicity of the writer/illustrator above the quality of the story but is willing to give new writers a chance to be reviewed and reach children likely to be reassured by the story in a setting familiar to them.

Blurbs

A brief back cover, i.e., the blurb, helps to engage readers who are already intrigued by the book because it gives a peek into what your book is about. Though blurbs are often written in-house, authors are also advised to write their own blurb. In the case the author writes their own blurbs, it will be edited in-house.

Blurbs should be aimed at the age group of the readers. They need to be pithy, well-written, to not give too much away, and be in the tone of the story. Questions can be asked, but not necessarily answered as a way of enticement. Usually a publisher/editor will limit the lines available to an author. With educational material, the blurb is often aimed at the harried teacher, not the student.

Learning to become media worthy

The work of an articulate, average but media-worthy writer will attract more attention than a brilliant author who mumbles, presents badly and is unreliable. However, the writer is welcome to look unconventional to the stereotypical image of a children's book author providing they can speak entertainingly and to the point. Varied types of speaking will be required: autographing sessions, large groups, TV cameras and/or radio microphones. Some writers encourage an eccentric manner, but the writer would be wise not to go too 'over the top'. A little eccentricity is attractive, too many leads to oblivion.

Websites and social media

A website and social media presence is vital for a writer to keep up to date with markets, organisations and fellow creators internationally. It also creates an author profile for professional publicity and material, such as hi-res author PR photos, which only have to be uploaded once.

A website and social media accounts are useful for various reasons:

- It helps to profile links to existing works online.
- Makes it easier to contact overseas publishers.
- Contains all relevant PR information in the one place. This means current books are listed, talks, bios, agent, publishers and a contact email address links the writer to the publisher.
- Author profiles on social media platforms like Instagram provide an engaging and visually appealing way for writers to connect with their readers, offering a glimpse into their creative process, personal life, and the world that inspires their work.

- LinkedIn can be a valuable platform for authors who write for young people by enabling them to connect with potential collaborators, publishers and educators.
- Child fans are more inclined to Google, then browse to get background information on your books and email rather than write a letter. It also saves the author writing repetitive responses.
- Allows writers to present topical themes. An author may have written a number of publications around a subject which suddenly becomes topical e.g., written articles about Antarctica. Having a page devoted to all work by the author on that subject with links is saves time for everyone.

Fan letters

One of the facts of life for a children's author is fan letters. Some are fascinating or flattering. Others are a challenge in terms of time and energy:

> Dear Arfer,
>
> My techer says we have to write. What books have you writ? Please send me a bok what you writ.
>
> Jon

Different authors employ different methods of responding to readers' letters or emails. Some authors have answers to standard questions already entered on their website. 'Readers' letters peak after an author speaking tour, annual events like Children's Book Week, an author's birthday which is listed in several literary diaries, or if there's a new book out.

This is an example of a thoughtful letter which an author answered personally:

> Christopher from 'The Frequent Flyer Twins' series is my favourite character. I like drawing like he does. But I also collect sports cards like Amy. I like basketball best. How do you decide which airport they will visit next? Did you know all about smuggling birds and reptiles before you wrote 'False Bottom' or did you find out? Who

did you ask? Could you have one of the stories happen at a country airfield like the one near us? When does the TV series start? Will Christopher be an actor or a cartoon character?

Love from Sara

Children's authors and illustrators get much more mail than adult writers, who often do NOT reply. Sometimes it's not possible to respond in the way the letter writer might like.

> I chose you for my author project. Send everything about you. I need a photo too. Jack

If you have connections or know teachers, it's best to recommend some advice that they can give to students who are junior readers:

- Actually read the author's works, rather than ask 'What have you written?'
- Ask thoughtful questions about specific books, characters or themes. All authors agree that 'Where do you get your ideas?' is the most commonly asked question.
- If all students in a class write a variation of the theme letter which the teacher drafted on the board, then expect to get one response in return, addressed to the class.
- Allow time for a response. Often letters are addressed to the publisher and take time to be re-routed to the author who may be in transit working nationally or internationally. Many authors answer their letters weekly, while others answer immediately.
- Avoid putting in a copy of the teacher's assignment and expect the author to shape an A plus project in response.
- Respond genuinely, even if critical of the book, as it shows that the reader has taken time to think about the story.
- Provide a return address, date and contact person. Several authors have spent time tracking down 'anonymous' but distressed students with assignment deadlines 'yesterday' and no return address.

Not Just a Piece of Cake: Being an Author by Hazel Edwards has a chapter on fan mail.

Writer-on-location

Once published, chances are an author will be invited to teach/lecture/workshop somewhere. The requirements vary enormously. Often a university or tertiary institution only requires that the writer be available on campus to comment informally on students' creative writing. An office is provided and it is acceptable for the writer to continue with their own writing. In return the writer's accommodation, living and travelling expenses are covered, plus a fee paid for the writer's time.

Community groups often require much more travelling, manuscript attention and diplomacy by the writer. Though writers are often shy, preferring to deal one on one, they can be expected to handle large audiences who are often a long way apart, as arts funding organisation tend to favour remote communities.

Really interesting locations can include jails, islands, remote communities, Antarctica, historic houses, mining settlements, and emergency organisations such as the police or fire brigade. An author maybe invited to draw attention to a location, to instil a sense of community or to support local arts.

Exercises

1. Write a letter to a funding organisation in support of the community which wants you to be a writer-on-location.
   a. What can you offer to this community?
   b. Over what period of time?
   c. What writing project will be completed collaboratively?
   d. What motivates this community?
   e. What do you hope to achieve?
   f. What will it cost? Their budget? What is your fee, expenses, travelling etc., productions costs of the writing project?
2. Image if someone approaches you with a very vague idea of a writing project in which they wish you to be involved. Perhaps some semi-medical organisation wants to involve you in a series of stories or a charitable event.
   a. How would you ask them to define the project?
   b. What is your time commitment?
   c. Is there a fee attached or are you being expected to do this for nothing? Suggests a case for an appropriate fee.
   d. Is a committee involved on decisions/quality/length of what is being done? Suggest ways of having more control.
   e. Is the deadline realistic?
   f. Are you expected to be the editor or the writer, or both?
   g. Practice saying 'no' or a qualified 'yes'.

Checklist

1. How personally do you take criticism? Do you see it as a critique of you or a helpful comment on your work?

_____
_____
_____
_____

2. Write your own blurb for your book. If you have difficulty doing this, maybe you need to reread your MS.

   _____

   _____

3. Take an objective look at yourself. How do you present? Is your appearance appropriate?

   _____

   _____

4. Have you practiced reading aloud? Find ways to get comfortable.

   _____

   _____

5. Do you allow other people to present their views, even if those views disagree with yours?

   _____

   _____

6. Do you have something interesting/innovative to say?

   _____

   _____

7. Do you take the time to answer fan mail?

   _____

   _____

8. Do you acknowledge your old writing friends?

   _____

   _____

CHAPTER 18

Agents and international sales

Literary agents

Two different writers can give very different answers when it comes to their personal experiences of working with agents:

1. *'My agent reads everything I write and makes terrific suggestions for improvement.'*
2. *'I've never managed to sell anything through an agent.'*

A literary agent is a person who represents the author in negotiations with publishers and the media. An agent can be a very useful 'front person' especially for a 'shy' author who is used to working quietly and alone. Because the agent is 'out there' in the marketplace, the agent is more likely to have up-to-date information about trends, possible commissions, and to suggest the author's name when requests come for screen adaptations, anthologies, newspaper profiles or participation in literary festivals.

Issues such as marketing to the most appropriate publisher, the wording of contract clauses, the size of advances, handling subsidiary rights which relate to selling the concept in other formats or other languages and even publicity may fall within the agent's brief. Many agents are also lawyers or at least have access to legal support. Usually there is a letter of agreement signed between the author and the agent. This may specify which titles the agent may handle.

In return, the agent receives a negotiated percentage of the author's royalties 'off the top' which is usually between 10–20% with occasional extra administrative charges. Either the agency will be international with branches in significant literary places such as London, Bologna in Italy and New York, or the agent will have a reciprocal arrangement with an overseas agent for the sale of international rights. In this case, the local agent may have to allow a percentage for the international agency. This may come out of the local agent's 15%.

The Catch-22 is that new writers who could most benefit from an agent's expertise, are not of financial interest to a literary agent. Since the agent's fee is directly linked to the author's income from royalties, it makes sense for the agent to concentrate on authors with a considerable back list of consistently selling titles, or those who are currently best-sellers. A new writer is unlikely to attract a good agent, until sales or talent are proven. It is a buyer's market for agents. Usually it is the agent who makes the approach, rather than the author.

In America, it has been mandatory to have an agent. But in Australia and New Zealand, many well-known and high-selling authors have handled their own literary negotiations without agents. With recent cutbacks in editorial staff amongst the major Australasian publishers of children's books, some publishers are insisting that they will accept only 'agented' material or manuscripts from their already published authors. This is partly a cost-cutting exercise to reduce the 'slush pile' reading required of their diminishing editorial staff. The practical result has been that literary agents are being required to 'sift' manuscripts before they reach the publishing house. Therefore, more writers and illustrators are seeking agents despite varied comments about the effectiveness of agents, especially from those with poor or spasmodic sales.

Some well-established authors do not have agents. Often this is because they:

- Enjoy negotiating with publishers.
- Are highly experienced at reading crucial contract clauses.
- Are prolific or have multiple interests and want to make a quick decision on a project, rather than waiting for an agent to respond.
- Have sufficient reputation for publishers to approach them or read their material.
- Do not want to pay the commission.

- Have a considerable backlist of titles they want to manage personally.
- Tend to rely on their publishers to handle sales of international rights or translations within their multi-national companies.

On the other hand, those with agent's value:

- Project book management across several publishers.
- Monitoring of royalty accounts.
- Placement with the most appropriate publisher with the best terms rather than routinely offering to an existing or previous publisher.
- Attention to subsidiary rights such as film, TV, multimedia or anthologising, eBooks, audiobooks and digital rights are significant negotiating areas.
- An advocate in the marketplace while author is writing.
- Emotional and critical support.
- Serendipitous happenings as a result of being in that agent's stable e.g., being asked to contribute to a collection, participate in a festival, or be a 'writer in residence'.
- Agented material is read by a publisher ahead of unsolicited.

So, it's wise for a first-time author to check all contract clauses and to seek advice from professional organisations like the Australian Society of Authors (ASA). They often offer 'Literary Speed Dating' events with agents and publishers where the author pays to pitch. This also happens at some literary festivals run by organisations like The Society of Children's Book Writers and Illustrators (SCBWI). It's also wise for a more experienced author to learn some basic contract law. Or approach an agent to handle the single book project only.

International sales

If a writer publishes one book a year, local sales are rarely enough to live on because of the small Australasian market where less than 3,000 copies may be an initial print run. Local sales are the 'bread and butter' while international sales mean the 'hundreds and thousands' and justify the amount of time spent on producing a quality book.

Whether seen as a 'bonus' or a necessity, book sales into other countries mean an author gains additional exposure, prestige and additional royalties without having to do further work on the manuscript. Sometimes changes in terminology need to be made for the American market. e.g., 'faucets' instead of 'taps'. Occasionally an international sale may be dependent upon the author changing an ending, or an incident and the ethical decision then rests with the author.

Some books are pre-sold into other English reading markets such as Canada, USA or parts of Asia. Often co-editions are agreed between publishers from different countries, and this increases the print run but also reduces the book unit cost.

Complications can arise with e-rights which are not restricted to any geographic area. So once e-rights are sold, other print publishers may not be interested if the electronic version can already be bought in their territory.

Translations and foreign rights

Other books have to be translated, and re-printed which is an additional cost. Some foreign 'runs' are very small perhaps 1,000 copies, while others may be aimed at the mass market. Seeing one's work translated into another language in a bound book is a special thrill that can't be replicated.

Translations are arranged by the publishing house. At the annual International Book Fairs in Bologna in Italy (April), and Frankfurt in Germany (October) buyers and sellers of international books meet to trade foreign rights. A book which has a gold award sticker is more likely to attract international interest, translations and co-editions, especially with Asian publishers. However, some subjects appeal universally, while others have only local interest.

Sale of rights can also relate to streaming services like Netflix, film or TV options, or producing the story in an innovative format. These subsidiary rights need careful negotiation as a new author, thrilled at the flattering attention, can naively sign away future possibilities for their 'hot' property. Realistically, many options are bought which never make it to the screen due to funding, scripting or distribution problems.

However, the author is entitled to keep the advance, even if the project never 'gets up', so when percentages are paid, it's wise to have a proportion paid upfront on signing of the contract rather than deferred until completion of the project. Major writers' organisations offer members contractual advice on international sales and subsidiary rights and have relevant articles available. A professional writing organisation is a professional tax deduction. In difficult circumstances they will act legally on behalf of members.

Other subsidiary rights relate to book club sales. Children's book clubs often make an offer for a title and will produce paperback editions which are sold at a much lower price than the recommended retail price (RRP) often in schoolbook clubs. Authors appreciate the exposure, but often the royalties on these subsidiary rights are very low.

Problems can also arise if the paperback edition of the book club is available at the same time as the more costly hardback produced by the original publisher. Obviously, parents and librarians tend to buy the cheaper edition, and this undercuts the hardback sales and full royalties to be paid to the author. Instead, the author receives the much lower royalties from the book club. So it's wise for a first-time author to check all contract clauses and to seek advice. It's also wise for a more experienced author to learn some basic contract law.

Works which travel well

The ideal international children's book is one which has a genuine but unique story offering the opportunity for readers from any culture to emotionally identify, and it is also artistically well produced. Certain types of children's books tend to be attractive to foreign publishers. Cultural differences are seen as 'educative' unless they are overwhelmingly different for the local reader. Currently Indigenous stories by Indigenous artists are popular, as are 'environmental' themes. Picture books often travel more easily and rely heavily on the artwork to convey the story internationally. Picture book apps are also seeing new trends having crossing languages.

For junior readers aged between 8-12, 'multicultural' stories are in demand, but the combinations of cultures required in the diverse illustrations and text may vary.

Humour relates to the tone in which something is written or said. Sometimes certain types of humour are not understood in other cultures. Some Australian 'tall stories' do not sell well in the USA nor in the UK.

Merchandising

Merchandising is often tied to a character or to a series. Merchandising covers toys, stationery, clothing and collectibles like stickers, badges, or mugs. Licensing rights are big business. Often the illustrator will be required to draw a range of poses for prospective licensees, who pay for the use of the character on their product. Contractual arrangements for the percentage of rights payable to various creators such as author, illustrator, designer, agent, publisher etc. can become very complicated.

If the writer is anticipating a major demand for a certain character, it's wise to retain control of subsidiary rights and negotiate them individually. Or use an agent.

Electronic rights and IP

The issue of electronic rights and intellectual property (IP) are becoming increasingly complex. Sometimes, merchandising agents want to take on a known book character, other times they want a new character which is unencumbered by prior agreements and permissions which have already been leased or assigned. Agreeing to a limited time contract or non-exclusive rights is another option and as time passes, generative AI will serve to create challenges and present new copyright issues.

Professional help

A writer may reach a stage where it becomes appropriate to employ the services of professionals mentioned earlier to help in your business of creativity. Don't forget that certain writers' organisations, offer assistance, but some forms of legal and specialised help are available only to their members.

Exercises

1. Reflect on your journey and the progress you've made as an author. List down the areas that you need improvement in and discern if hiring a literary agent is necessary to help you cover these areas.
2. Challenge yourself to be familiar with the ins-and-outs of the publishing and legal process, especially if you work without a literary agent.
3. Search for children's books written by international authors. Note down what is different compared to local competitors and what makes them stand out.

Checklist

1. Do you need a literary agent to assist you with negotiation and to handle the non-writing aspects?

   _____

   _____

2. Do you enjoy dealing with publishers yourself? What have you learned from your own personal experiences and how can you improve future meetings with publishers?

   _____

   _____

   _____

   _____

3. Have you considered signing up for writers' organisations such as ASA and SCBWI?

   _____

   _____

4. Have you read any international children's books?

5. Have you researched any noticeable trends for translated children's books?

6. Have you read any books that focuses on a 'multicultural' story?

7. Consider what type of merchandising will be most suitable for your own book.

8. Look through what writers' organisations or what professional authors are saying or dealing with AI. List down what you can learn from them.

GLOSSARY

The A to Z of writing for young people

A. Audience: Your reading clients. Know their needs and interests.
B. Business plan: Where your writing is aimed, how and why.
C. Cash flow: Inwards, as well as outwards.
D. Dialogue: A technique to make your characters live.
E. Editor: A valued colleague.
F. Freelance: Originally a medieval mercenary. Fee for service.
G. Ghost writer: Author of a work for someone else.
H. Home office: Reduces travel time.
I. IQ: People mistakenly assume children's authors' IQ is equivalent to the age of their child reader.
J. Journalistic skills: Helpful for junior non-fiction.
K. Knowledge of market is vital: Tailor your work to them.
L. Literature: What you are creating?
M. Multimedia: That multidefined portfolio you need to know to stay up to date.
N. Network: Peer support.
O. Originality: Sets you apart.
P. Persistence: Major trait for a published writer.
Q. Quit? Never.

R. Rights: Be aware of which ones you are signing away.
S. Series: The successful development of a concept.
T. Titles: Take time to think of apt ones.
U. Understanding: Deepens empathy, drives compelling storytelling.
V. Voice: Captivates readers, distinguishes your work.
W. Website: Your international shopfront.
X. Unknown: The creative challenge of making something out of one idea.
Y. Young Adult (YA) fiction: Often exploring themes of growth and self-discovery.
Z. Zest: A necessary ingredient if writing for children, with enjoyment.

Appendix

Tips for school students writing their own books

Embarking on the journey of writing one's own book is a remarkable endeavor, especially for school students. It's a creative outlet that allows them to express their thoughts, imagination, and unique perspectives in a tangible form. However, crafting a book, whether it's a novel, a collection of short stories, or even a non-fiction work, can be a challenging and rewarding process. In this age of digital information and constant distractions, young authors face a set of unique challenges. Yet, with the right guidance and strategies, they can turn their literary aspirations into reality.

Many school students, school staff and families want to write their own 'history of our school' book. Individual students are also keen to share their personal stories through writing. This act of self-expression is a creative outlet that allows them to explore their unique experiences, perspectives and voices. It can be a means of reflection, self-discovery, and empowerment. In addition, publishing their stories can inspire and resonate with others, fostering a sense of camaraderie and understanding within the school community.

Here are some tips to get you started:

- Who is going to read it? Write in a way which interests them e.g., visuals, maps, photos, cartoons, diagrams, samples, recipes.
- What's the most interesting thing which has gone wrong in your life? What are you most proud of?
- Contrast then and now. Old & new ways? What did grandparents eat at school when they were kids? Subjects studied? How did you

learn without computers? What did they ride? Wear? Talk about in playground? Games?

- Structure. What are the most common questions people ask? Answer those. When? Where? Why? How? Who?
- Check your facts.
- Choose a title which is a clue to important things in the book.
- Expect to write several drafts.
- Check the spelling. Don't just use spellcheck.
- Edit it. Get someone else to edit it too.
- Design. Size? Number of pages? Colour? Print book or eBook?
- Expect it to take longer than you planned.
- Celebrate the completion or publication with a book lauch party.

A historical gift: Writing for children in your extended family

Writing a story can be a gift of the imagination, as well as a record of family times or history. Writing for children in the family can inspire young imaginations, cultivate a passion for reading, and build meaningful connections through storytelling. By crafting engaging stories tailored to the children's interests, you can instill important values, spark curiosity, and provide a source of lifelong joy and learning. Writing for the younger members of their family is their way of passing down the enchantment of storytelling from one generation to the next.

Here are some tips to get you started:

- Write around the family photos you already possess rather than start with the text.
- Include all family members in the action and photos.
- Choose a topic which interests that aged child and becomes part of their their story.
- Create a low-resolution digital format to email but print out copies too.

- Choose a slip-in folder or more elaborate binding.
- Create an apt title.
- Dedicate the book to the child.
- Write one sentence per visual. Use repetition.
- Aim for an easy reading rhythm. Test by reading aloud.
- Don't forget, a twist for the end.

Some optional extras worth considering:

- You can make the story WITH the child. Or for an older relative's significant birthday e.g., a relative's 60th birthday.
- Add a collage of 'feelie' bits.
- Use a contrasting story of then and now, for a family event e.g., starting school. Contrast photos from your schooldays.
- Make a few copies for extended family.

About the author

An avid reader (who read under the bedclothes as a young girl), Hazel Edwards wrote her first novel in grade six, a mystery about adventurous children stuck in a mine. After working in a secondary school and lecturing at Teachers' College, Hazel published her first novel aged twenty-seven, *General Store*.

It is Hazel's third published work that is her best known, the children's picture book classic, *There's a Hippopotamus on Our Roof Eating Cake*. This special imaginary friend has been cherished by children and parents alike and led to the dubious honour of Hazel being referred to as 'the Hippo Lady'.

Since its publication in 1980, the age-less Hippopotamus on the roof has been reprinted annually, evolved into a series of seven picture books, inspired a junior chapter book, classroom play scripts, a musical stage production and a short movie. The Hippopotamus books have also been translated into Mandarin, Braille, Auslan and were presented as an official Australian Government gift to the children of Princess Mary of Denmark.

Whilst Hazel loves creating quirky, feisty characters for newly independent readers in her easy-to-read junior chapter books (such as *Sleuth Astrid: The mind-reading chook*), she writes for all ages and has published over 220 books across a range of subjects and genres.

Hazel has collaborated with experts to publish adult non-fiction titles such as such as *Difficult Personalities* (now translated into seven languages), helps people craft memoirs and family histories by *Writing a Non-Boring Family History* and co-wrote *f2m:the boy within*.

Awarded the Australian Antarctic Division Arts Fellowship in 2001, Hazel travelled to Casey Station on the Polar Bird. This visit inspired a range of creative projects including the young adult eco-mystery *Antarctica's Frozen Chosen*, picture book *Antarctic Dad* and the memoir *Antarctic Writer on Ice*.

A fan of interesting and unusual locations, Hazel has been a guest writer-in-residence at the former Fremantle Prison (now the Fremantle Children's Literature Centre), the Mount Newman mining community in outback WA, a visiting author to Pasir Ridge International School in Indonesia and an author ambassador to Youfu West Street International School in Nanjing, China.

Passionate about literacy and creativity, Hazel has proudly held the title of Reading Ambassador for various organisations. Formerly a director on the Committee of Management of the Australian Society of Authors, Hazel was awarded an OAM for Literature (2013) and Monash University awarded her the Distinguished Alumni for Education (2022). Currently she is patron of the Society of Women Writers (Vic).

Hazel writes a new story for her four grandsons each birthday.

In 2024, Hazel is celebrating a Golden Anniversary, 50 years since her first book published.

www.ingramcontent.com/pod-product-compliance
Lightning Source LLC
Chambersburg PA
CBHW052140110526
44591CB00012B/1796